A History of
FRANKLIN COUNTY
NORTH CAROLINA

A History of
FRANKLIN COUNTY
NORTH CAROLINA

Eric Medlin

THE
History
PRESS

Published by The History Press
Charleston, SC
www.historypress.com

Copyright © 2020 by Eric Medlin
All rights reserved

First published 2020

Manufactured in the United States

ISBN 9781467143653

Library of Congress Control Number: 2020932100

CONTENTS

PREFACE

In 1808, the young diarist Edward Hooker traveled through Franklin County and produced one of the first written descriptions of the town of Louisburg. He was not impressed by the town's shabby dwellings or its surrounding barren lands. Hooker had seen too much of Connecticut and the prosperous areas of South Carolina to think highly of what the county had to offer at this early date. However, Hooker was impressed by Matthew Dickinson, the leader of the town's academy, and remarked on the role that transportation might play in the county's future. Hooker noted that the entire county, Louisburg in particular, was in close proximity to the Tar River. He reported the belief of Dickinson and other local citizens that the river was "capable of being rendered navigable." A navigable Tar River would connect the county with the much larger town of Tarboro to the east, then to the Atlantic Ocean. This was the only possibility that Hooker observed for the town to eventually grow and become successful.

Fast forward to 2020—a much different time for the United States and the world—and the country has a knowledge-based economy, dominated by the internet, service jobs and car travel. With the exception of the Tar River and a few remaining buildings, the county looks nothing like the place Edward Hooker visited; yet, the most recent news story to include Franklin County focused on transportation, specifically the decision to increase funding for the widening of U.S. Route 401 between Louisburg and the bustling state capital of Raleigh.[1] Instead of connecting to Tarboro, the road will connect with Raleigh, which is seen by outside observers as the key to making Franklin County successful.

The story of Franklin County is often one of transportation, geographical relationships and proximity. Franklin County began as a site farther west of most Tuscarora towns and the earliest European settlements. It became the poorer, southern companion of Warren County, sharing a tobacco culture and even some of the same families and plantation home architects. Then, Franklin County was defined by its relationship to Raleigh and other stops on the area's railroads and highways. A plausible story of the county—especially its towns of Franklinton and Louisburg and its northern plantations—over the past three centuries can be told through these many relationships.

Focusing on the county as a foil for its neighbors, a railway stop or a suburb misses so much of what makes Franklin County unique. A set of unique geographic, social and economic circumstances helped produce a surprisingly advanced and developed rural county. Towns like Louisburg and Franklinton developed their own institutions, including leading centers of education and industry. Architects, artisans and poets created historically significant works of art that must be understood on their own merit. The county produced several political leaders apart from the trends in Warrenton and Raleigh. It is Franklin County's mix of many influences and its refusal to be defined simply as a tobacco center or as a county of cotton markets and furniture factories that make it such a worthy subject of historical inquiry.

This book deals with Franklin County's structures, people and role in history, from the pre-European era to the present day. Franklin County's story is undoubtedly one of success. Franklin County has been one of the wealthiest counties in the state for many years of its existence; it has attracted visits from governors, senators and a plethora of congressmen. Its educational institutions have won accolades and hired national talents. The county has even been able to reinvent itself over the past four decades—since the beginnings of deindustrialization—and it seems poised to carry on this level of success like few of its fellow counties in the eastern Piedmont region.

However, a number of people missed out on the county's largesse. A large percentage of the county's residents (in some years, the majority of them) were enslaved for much of the eighteenth and nineteenth centuries. Following Reconstruction, the county's African Americans were subject to discrimination, segregation and acts of political violence—including lynching. The county's women and Native Americans also suffered poor treatment. It was not until the later years of the twentieth century that these

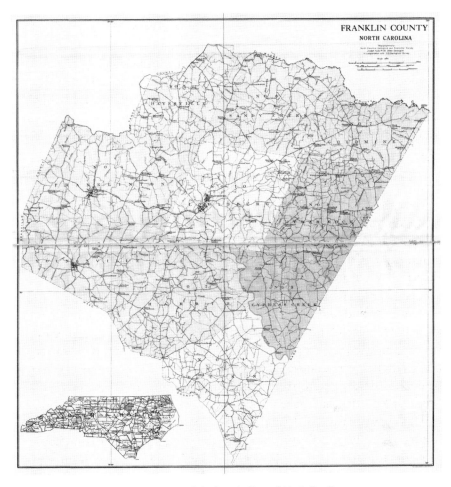

Franklin County map, 1907. *Courtesy of the State Archives of North Carolina.*

groups were able to start taking political power and become full citizens of Franklin County. A study of the county's history, even a brief one, must take their experiences into account in order to have any chance of telling the full, rich story that incorporates all of the county's citizens.

ACKNOWLEDGEMENTS

I have many people to thank for the formation of this book. My great thanks go out to the men and women of Franklin County, who helped provide context, information and paths forward for my work. Pat Hinton, Robert Radcliffe, Holt Kornegay and Scott Mumford aided in the research process. Joseph A. Pearce Jr. and Maurice York, two of Franklin County's most distinguished historians, reviewed my manuscript and provided me with helpful comments and feedback. Vann Evans and Erin Fulp at the North Carolina State Archives, along with Dr. Mary Beth Fitts at the North Carolina Office of State Archaeology, helped me with research, along with the staff at the North Carolina Collection at the University of North Carolina at Chapel Hill. I also received help with images and copyright permissions from the staff members at *Our State* magazine and the Library of Congress. My special thanks go to Joe Mobley, for giving me the idea to write a county history, and to Michael R. Hill, Michael Coffey and Dr. James Crisp, for guiding my early research. Finally, I would like to thank Susan C. Rodriguez for her extensive help in editing my manuscript at every stage of the process and my mother, Julia Medlin, for inspiring me throughout my life.

BEGINNINGS TO THE REVOLUTION

Franklin County, North Carolina, is located in North Carolina's Piedmont region of rolling hills and fertile soil. The county is the forty-fifth-largest county in North Carolina, containing 491.68 square miles of land and 2.82 square miles of water.[2] Its topography and soil type are typical of most eastern Piedmont counties. The highest point in the county—at 561 feet—is located west of the town of Youngsville. The most common type of soil found in the county is Wedowee-Helena; it is a well-draining form of soil, with a loamy surface layer and a subsoil composed mostly of clay. Wedowee-Helena is found primarily in the interior part of the county, along broad ridges and slopes. This soil can grow a number of crops including corn, tobacco, soybeans, sorghum and cotton. Another common soil type in the area, Wake-Wedowee-Wateree, is characterized by its exceptional ability to drain water and its presence on modest slopes. The county's large amount of fertile soil, combined with its few tall ridges and swamplands, have made it a center for agriculture throughout its history.

Franklin County's soil and temperate climate determine the composition of its forests. Loblolly pines are prevalent in the county's forests, along with white pines and beech, hickory and oak trees. These trees are good for forestry and milling, but they are not useful for the naval stores industry that buoyed the North Carolina economy in its early years. Franklin County has also had a wide variety of mineral wealth throughout its history. The county's rocks held considerable gold veins, and they were most prominently explored in the nineteenth and twentieth centuries in the Portis Gold Mine, a mine near the present-day community of Wood. Other minerals extracted in Franklin County over the past three centuries have included mica and gemstones.[3]

While the topography and flora of Franklin County are similar to those of other nearby counties, one unique aspect of the county is its large amount of fresh water. The county is traversed by a considerable number of rivers and creeks. Several of Franklin County's creeks, including Lynch Creek and Cedar Creek, are over ten miles long, and they eventually drain into either the Tar or Little River. These creeks are fueled by the average forty-five inches of rain that the county receives each year.[4] The county's porous soil also creates many aquifers that can be easily tapped by wells. Springs abound in the county, and they were often attractions for the county's historic settlements. Reports suggest that Franklin County has been known for its numerous sources of fresh water since the eighteenth century.

The most prominent waterway in the county is the Tar River. The Tar is North Carolina's second-longest river located completely inside the state, trailing only the nearby Neuse. It runs for a total of 215 miles, beginning in Person County and ending in Washington, North Carolina, where it becomes the Pamlico River. The Tar River bisects Franklin County, entering near the town of Franklinton, along the county border, and leaving just outside of Lake Royale. While the Tar has been a source of power and fishing for the residents of Franklin County for centuries, it has not been helpful for large-scale navigation. The entirety of Franklin County lies upstream of the Tar River's fall line, a region of rocks and falls near present-day Rocky Mount that hinder navigation between the Piedmont and the Atlantic Ocean. The river is not navigable throughout the entire county; it is too narrow and is shallow enough to be forded at several points. The Tar River dries up to a trickle during times of drought at its lowest points in the county.

Franklin County's location in the Piedmont region and its abundant waterways made it an attractive area for Native American settlement. Native Americans first entered the Piedmont region of North Carolina around twelve thousand years ago; by the seventeenth century, several groups had settled in the areas to the north and east of the Tar River, toward the Roanoke River. Native groups, including the Saponi and Moratok, hunted and fished in the region's rivers, like the Tar, and grew corn on the region's fertile land.[5] The Saponi were a Siouan-speaking people; they were closely related to the Eno and Shakori peoples, who lived in what are now Wake, Orange and Durham Counties.

The Tar River, as seen from the Bickett Boulevard bridge. *Original photograph taken by the author.*

In the centuries leading up to the year 1600, the Iroquoian-speaking Tuscarora became the dominant power in the region. The Tuscarora came from what is now upstate New York and had moved into present-day North Carolina by 600 CE. They formed a number of towns and forts throughout the region around Franklin County. Typical Tuscarora towns in the Franklin County area consisted of longhouses, central plazas and outlying farms. The Tuscarora subsisted on the corn they grew, and they hunted in nearby forests, primarily deer for the deerskin trade. Northern Tuscarora towns were well-fortified to protect against attacks from other Native American groups.[6] Known Tuscarora towns and forts included Catechna, Nooherooka and Tasqui. In the eighteenth century, many of the towns closest to Franklin County were part of the northern federation led by Chief Tom Blount, a Tuscarora leader who was friendlier to the English than his southern counterparts.

The Tuscarora and other Native Americans in the Franklin County area were greatly affected by the arrival of Europeans. By 1700, English settlements had sprung up throughout Virginia, coastal South Carolina and the area east of the Chowan River in North Carolina. Virginians began to populate North Carolina in the 1650s, bringing their culture of corn cultivation and tobacco plantations with them. English settlers particularly in South Carolina became wealthy through trade with the Catawba and other groups. Trade helped facilitate the wealth of numerous native peoples in the vicinity of Franklin County, including the Tuscarora. Native Americans throughout the area traded deerskin and furs for copper implements, iron tools and guns. The Catawba and the Tuscarora also practiced the Native American slave trade throughout North and South Carolina.

European settlers and Native Americans increasingly used the Great Trading Path, a trail that stretched through neighboring Warren and Granville Counties, for commerce. The Great Trading Path was facilitated by the Occoneechee, a Siouan-speaking people closely related to the Eno and the Saponi. This path was just one of many routes that crisscrossed the North Carolina Piedmont region in the late seventeenth and early eighteenth centuries. Another contemporaneous trail called Green's Path connected southeast Virginia and northeast North Carolina with the Franklin County area in the mid-eighteenth century.[7] These paths helped spread European crafts, weapons and diseases. As in other parts of the New World, European diseases had killed a large percentage of the Native Americans who lived in the vicinity of Franklin County before the first permanent white settlers had even arrived.

Pioneering North Carolina explorer John Lawson reached an area near Franklin County in his travels across the colony. In 1700, Lawson left Charles Town, South Carolina (present-day Charleston), to explore the interiors of North and South Carolina. Lawson wrote of some waterfalls that he stopped by near the end of his travels; he described one as having "mighty rocks, the water making a strange noise as if a great many water-mills were going at once."[8] It is generally accepted that this location was either the Falls of the Neuse (seven miles southwest of Franklin County) or the Falls of the Little River (eleven miles south of Franklin County).

During his travels, Lawson noticed the swift rivers, generally flat pine woods and marble outcrops of the region, describing them as "a good range for cattle, though very indifferent for swine."[9] He also mentioned large numbers of Tuscarora in the region of the falls, including several towns and a group of five hundred Tuscarora hunters. Lawson's trek from the falls took him to the present-day site of Washington, a future port city at the mouth of the Tar-Pamlico River, and he concluded his journey at North Carolina's first incorporated town, Bath. Lawson's travelogue, the first English description of the North Carolina interior, became an influential text in promoting the English settlement of the North Carolina Piedmont region.

In 1711, tensions between the Tuscarora and expanding European colonial settlements escalated into all-out war. Tuscarora leaders killed John Lawson and launched an attack that burned the town of Bath to the ground. North Carolinians solicited help from South Carolina militias; the first was led by John Barnwell, and a later group was led by James Moore. Along with Native American allies and North Carolina militia leaders, the English defeated the Tuscarora and burned several of their towns and forts; they destroyed Fort Nooherooka (located thirty eight miles south of Franklin County, in present-day Greene County) and killed its 558 inhabitants.[10] The English took 392 prisoners as slaves, and they were later sold by the English and their allies, including the South Carolina Yemassee. The northern Tuscarora who supported the English were moved to the Indian Woods Reservation in present-day Bertie County. The remaining Tuscaroras later left the region to rejoin the Iroquois in New York, where they became the Sixth Tribe of the Iroquois.

Around the same time, most of the non-Tuscarora Native Americans near Franklin County, such as the Saponi, felt pressure from both European settlers in Virginia and the surrounding Native American groups. In 1714, Virginia governor Alexander Spotswood offered to give these groups refuge at Fort Christanna, which was located just over the Virginia border. The Saponi left North Carolina and joined many other Algonquin-speaking peoples in the fort. They remained there for four years before the fort was closed, and they eventually returned to present-day Warren and Halifax Counties in North Carolina.

The end of the Tuscarora War fundamentally altered the pattern of English growth and settlement in North Carolina, as North Carolinians began settling west of the Chowan River after the war. The most prominent movement occurred along the Neuse and Cape Fear Rivers. Colonists established tobacco plantations on land that had been either abandoned by or taken from the Tuscarora. The settlers established Cape Fear port towns, such as Newton (now Wilmington) and Brunswick Town, which shifted the population center of the colony southward. Smaller groups of colonists began to settle along the Pamlico and Tar Rivers. By 1726, they had reached the area near the present-day town of Tarboro (located thirty-three miles east of Franklin County). This gradual westward movement continued for the rest of the eighteenth century.

There is evidence that a decade after the end of the war, another conflict that possibly involved the Tuscaroras occurred in Franklin County. An archaeological site in the central part of Franklin County contains a mound with evidence of a Native American village. Since the nineteenth century, at the latest, there has been a local legend that this Lynch Creek mound was the site of the last battle of the Tuscarora War. The legend states that a group of Tuscarora were chased to a site between Lynch Creek and the Tar River.[11] A flooded creek prevented them from fleeing farther, and they were massacred on the banks of the creek by a group of colonial militia. The massacre was said to have been so large that there were piles of skeletons in the mound—so many that anatomy students visited the site to procure bones for their studies. This story has persisted in local histories to the present day; it was even mentioned in the 1930s Works Progress Administration guide to North Carolina.[12]

It is indeed possible that a massacre of some scale occurred at the alleged site. Around the two years that local historians have given for the massacre (1723 and 1725), the Tuscarora occasionally attacked white settlers. There is abundant evidence of Native American settlement in the local area, and prehistoric spear points, atlatl and soapstone have been discovered near Lynch Creek.[13] But apart from the writings of local historians and recollections of skeletons near the banks of Lynch Creek, there is no substantial evidence—documented or otherwise—of this massacre.

Even after the end of the war, the area now known as Franklin County was not to be settled by Europeans for several decades. The earliest nearby European intervention occurred in 1728, when a patent was granted to North Carolina leader Edward Moseley by King George II. Moseley was a member of the royal council and an instigator of numerous controversies and conflicts throughout the early years of the colony.[14] He was also a surveyor and created one of the earliest maps of the colony, now known as the *Moseley Map*, in 1728. Like other North Carolina leaders at the time, Moseley became an absentee landowner of several large estates throughout the Piedmont region of the colony. His most famous plantations were located in the Cape Fear River Valley, but Moseley also owned a massive estate in the vicinity of Franklin County. This estate, which was named Clun Seat after a river in England, was located on the northern border, between present-day Warren and Franklin Counties.[15] It was later broken up and sold to a number of families in the 1740s.

An early group of settlers also reached the area immediately north of Franklin County in the early 1730s. William Duke and Gideon Macon both settled in the area near the present-day northern boundary of Franklin County, on Shocco Creek, in the 1730s. Duke and Macon planted tobacco and quickly accumulated a modest amount of wealth—enough to build houses with windows.[16] They were later joined by other settlers in the region north of Shocco Creek, up to the Virginia border. As for the area south of Clun Seat and Shocco Creek, it was too remote and removed from the navigable portion of the Tar River to attract European settlement prior to the 1730s.

By 1735, the colony of North Carolina had begun to stabilize. The English Crown took over most of the colony in 1729, and it was ruled by a number of successful governors, such as Gabriel Johnston and Arthur Dobbs. Tobacco cultivation continued to be the primary mode of economic growth, and the success of the colony attracted more immigrants. At the same time powerful Native American groups were either pushed westward or eliminated entirely by fighting forces. Soon, colonists began to trickle into the territory that is now Franklin County, and the same factors that made the county a successful site for Native American cultivation also made it a prosperous area for colonists.

COLONIAL AND REVOLUTIONARY BEGINNINGS

1715–1783

The first Europeans to settle in what is now Franklin County arrived three decades after the end of the Tuscarora War, back when the area was still part of Edgecombe and Granville Counties. Most of these early settlers had been in the nearby areas of Virginia and North Carolina for decades prior to their arrivals. Throughout the seventeenth and early eighteenth centuries, large planters purchased much of the most fertile land in southeastern Virginia and northeastern North Carolina. Most of the new settlers in these colonies, who had arrived in the New World seeking land and tobacco profits, were greatly disappointed by the amount of land that was available and the possibilities of indentured servitude that awaited them. Large plantation owners dominated the local political systems and social structures. Economic and social conditions soon pushed new arrivals out of the areas near the Atlantic Ocean, the Albemarle Sound and the mouth of the James River. Around the same time, the defeat of the Tuscarora Native Americans opened up large swaths of the tribe's fertile land to European settlement.

Europeans began steadily moving south and west in the decades after 1715, following the course of the area's major rivers, including the Roanoke, Neuse and Tar Rivers. The settlers in this region applied for and received large land grants from either the English Crown or the Earl of Granville (for land north of latitude line 35°34'). In 1743, the governor's council granted 200 acres of land south of Sandy Creek, which cuts through the middle of present-day Franklin County, to John Terrell.

Several more grants were made in 1749, including one for 2,500 acres to Giles Bowers, another for 330 acres to Osborne Jeffreys and another for 200 acres to Edward Jones. Settlers began building plantations and homesteads on many of Franklin County's current waterways, including Cedar Creek, Crooked Creek, Lynch Creek and Lyons Creek.

Several of the buildings that were constructed by the earliest Franklin County families remain standing in the area. One prominent example is the home of the Perry family. In 1752, Jeremiah Perry received a grant from the Earl of Granville for 382 acres in the vicinity of Cedar Creek, which runs through the middle of present-day Franklin County. Perry and his siblings built a one-story house, which they named Cascine after a popular horseracing park in Florence, Italy.[17] The Perry family, like the other families in the area, lived by farming and raising hogs, sheep and cows for food and clothing. The family's other major crops, corn and tobacco, were grown to be sold, but sending goods to market was difficult. The Tar River, one of North Carolina's largest rivers, flowed just a few miles north of the Perry plantation, but it was too small and laden with too many obstacles to be navigable. As a result, the settlers had to haul their goods by wagon, either north, into Virginia, or south, to distant towns like Cross Creek, to be sold.

Cascine (mid-eighteenth century), one of the oldest buildings still standing in Franklin County. *Courtesy of the Library of Congress.*

Like other early settlers who were wealthy, Perry owned slaves. The 1790 census mentions that several slaves lived on the Cascine property and that over one hundred slaves were owned by Perry family members. Slavery supplanted indentured servitude as a source of labor in the eighteenth century and defined Franklin County's economy and social structure until the end of the Civil War. In addition, the current land of the Perry Plantation contains evidence of a possible common pastime in the area: horseracing. Wills from the time period mentioned prized horses, and from an early point in Cascine's history, the family raced horses around a circle of oaks that still exists on the property.

The Shemuel Kearney House is also still standing, although it has been moved to Louisburg from its original location in the southwestern portion of the county. Kearney was a member of a prominent family in Halifax County, who moved to a piece of land on Cedar Creek that had previously been owned by Joseph Fuller. In 1758, he built a two-story house with a gambrel roof (a distinctive, symmetrical gable roof with four sides instead of two). The gambrel roof was an unusual feature in the area, where simple frame and log-built houses were prevalent. This architectural feature was much more common on the houses of wealthy residents in eastern towns like Edenton and New Bern. Its presence on a house in what was then the backcountry suggests that its builders were attempting to emulate the more refined eastern culture. The area around Kearney's plantation, later known as the town of Franklinton, eventually became another locus for settlement, along with the central and southeast sections of the county.[18]

The earliest families in what later became Franklin County were joined by more and more settlers throughout the 1750s and 1760s. Upon arriving, these settlers cleared land and established grist mills on creeks and rivers. Grist mills used waterpower to produce meal, sawed logs and other goods that could be used or sold at market. Families also operated stills to convert corn into liquor, a process that turned surplus corn into a consumer good.[19] Corn and tobacco farming remained the most common economic practices in the area throughout the colonial period. They were eventually supplemented by wheat, which was widespread throughout the North Carolina Piedmont region at the time. Families fished in the county's numerous creeks and in the Tar River. Men and women with varying degrees of wealth arrived, and the wealthiest brought their slaves. While slave-based plantations made up a bulk of the economy in the Franklin County area, the number of slaves on Franklin County plantations always remained relatively small when compared to the plantations in the coastal

Shemuel Kearney House (mid-eighteenth century), one of the oldest extant houses in the county. *Courtesy of the State Archives of North Carolina.*

plain. These early families also mostly lived in rural isolation; there were no towns in what is now Franklin County until 1779.

In the 1750s, just a few years after arriving in the area, the citizens of the eastern portion of Granville County began asking for better representation and a closer courthouse. A closer county courthouse would have made it easier for settlers to buy and sell land, handle legal disputes and file wills and petitions. By requesting a closer courthouse, the citizens of eastern Granville replicated a process that had been started several decades earlier, when settlers moved west and led to the formation of Bertie County, Edgecombe County and Granville County itself.

The colonial General Assembly's first response to these citizens rose from the relationship between the county's residents and the Church of England. Parishes (or local districts) of the Church of England were a fundamental part of life for residents throughout North Carolina, and they were a major tax expenditure and a center of political and social relations. In 1756, the General Assembly passed an act that provided more local church governance for the residents of what is now Franklin County. This act formed St. John's Parish, which was founded "where Jefferson's Road now crosses the Virginia line, running thence a direct line to Horse Creek, where Johnson County line crosses the said creek."[20] This new parish allowed for a more efficient tithe collection and a more immediate control of parish affairs through local vestrymen.

Ruins of a grist mill on the Tar River. *Original photograph taken by the author.*

In 1764, the General Assembly created a new county from St. John's Parish and named it for the Earl of Bute, an important adviser to King George III. The county's courthouse was to be located in an area known as Buffalo Race-Path (approximately thirty-five miles north of the southern border of present-day Franklin County). A year after its formation, a tax list prepared by the colonial General Assembly showed that Bute County had the sixth-largest population of the twenty-nine counties in the colony at that time.[21] Despite its initial success, the name Bute was a source of consternation throughout the county's short life. In 1765, just one year after the county's formation, the English Parliament passed the Stamp Act, which was an unprecedented direct tax on many of the documents that were essential to the business, legal and recreational activities of the colonists. The Stamp Act provoked a massive response, as colonists submitted petitions, rioted and attacked tax collectors. Lord Bute had been a prominent supporter of the act, and across the colonies, including in New Bern, mobs burned effigies of the royal adviser.

Bute County was founded to give greater representation to its citizens, but many citizens in the new county still felt ignored and slighted after 1764.

Citizens primarily felt this way because of the county's north–south divide. Citizens in the northern half of the county had settled several decades before those in the southern half. Many had come from Virginia in the two decades following William Byrd's expedition to survey the boundary between the two colonies. Families in the county's northern half had more money, larger plantations and a greater number of slaves. Some of the most prominent families in North Carolina in the eighteenth and nineteenth centuries came from the northern half of what was then Bute County. These families included the Macons, Hawkinses and Sumners, and they had easier access to the Roanoke River and the refined cities of eastern Virginia than southern Bute County landowners.

A greater concentration of wealth north of Shocco Creek led to more political clout for northern residents, which led to the county courthouse being placed closer to their plantations than those of southern residents. Many of the county's early representatives in the colonial General Assembly, including Thomas Bell and Benjamin Ward, mainly owned land in the county's northern half. The first complaint from the citizens of the southern half of Bute County came in 1764, when they issued a petition that argued that the courthouse should be moved closer to them.[22] Even with the wealth of the county's northern residents, the administration in Bute County was still primitive when compared to the standards of coastal North Carolina. Three years before Chowan County built its two-story brick courthouse in Edenton, Bute County held court in a tavern owned by one of its residents, Jethro Sumner. The courthouse was still located in Sumner's tavern when British traveler John F.D. Smyth visited North Carolina in the 1770s. Smyth described Sumner as an amiable host but one who could be prone to a "violent" demeanor.[23]

In 1768, four years after the founding of Bute County, its citizens found themselves swept up in the fervor of the Regulator movement. Backcountry farmers balked at how high their taxes were and how sparse their representation was when compared to the prominent planters of the east. The tax-funded construction of a massive new home for Royal Governor William Tryon, known as Tryon Palace, further inflamed these tensions. Farmers called themselves Regulators because they hoped to regulate their own circumstances. They began issuing petitions against Tryon and the General Assembly, attacking tax collectors and burning the homes of royal officials. In the Regulator movement, Bute County occupied a peculiar role. The county was firmly placed in the backcountry, and its citizens exhibited considerable anger against royal officials. Governor Tryon's plea to the county to send troops for the royal militia went unanswered. A local minister wrote that the Regulators in Bute County had "obstructed our courts of Justice, threatened the capital, destroyed several gentlemen's buildings, whip every officer who calls upon them for taxes, or if they seize their goods without interruption, they can't sell them for want of buyers, which is the case of our county."[24] The rallying cry of "there are no Tories in Bute County" came not from the Revolutionary War but from the county's reputation during the War of Regulation. At one point, discontent in the county was so strong that it fueled a rumor that a mob from Bute County was on its way to attack New Bern. In response, "the [governor's] council, trembling with terror, called out the Craven regiment to guard the town."[25]

At the same time, many of Bute County's most prominent citizens eventually did join with Governor Tryon to put down the rebellion. Alexander McCulloch, a prominent landowner in Bute County and a future clerk of court, marched with Tryon during his first attempt to stop the Regulators in 1768. Citizens who joined Tryon on his later Regulator campaigns included Philemon Hawkins and William Eaton (Hawkins as an aide-de-camp to Tryon and Eaton as a colonel).[26] Hawkins and his son joined Tryon on his march across North Carolina, meeting at New Bern and blazing a westward trail across the Piedmont region, to the heart of the Regulator movement in Orange County. They were probably present when the royal government shot at its own rebelling citizens at the Battle of Alamance. Eaton and Hawkins both came from the wealthier northern half of Bute County. None of the prominent families from southern Bute County attained such high ranks in the anti-Regulator campaign. The defeat of the Regulators at Alamance, which resulted in the deaths of nine Regulators and either the arrest or forced fleeing of the rest of their leaders, meant that the Regulator movement was no longer a significant military threat.

In the 1770s, American anger over British taxes, which was previously expressed through petitions and riots, erupted into open revolt. Rebels began organizing militias, gathering arms and crafting new governments across the thirteen colonies. North Carolina was no exception from this activity. In July 1775, an angry mob forced Royal Governor Josiah Martin to flee the colony for the safety of a British warship that was anchored near the Cape Fear River. North Carolinians followed the lead of other colonies and formed committees of safety and a provincial congress to govern their own territory. The nominally independent state also sent delegates to the Second Continental Congress in order to coordinate the war effort alongside the twelve other rebellious colonies.

Bute County and its inhabitants' early commitment to the American Revolution soon became well known. Jethro Sumner and Benjamin Hawkins became military leaders in the Patriot army. Sumner led troops and won distinction at the Battle of Stono Ferry, where Patriot forces attempted to take back Charleston, South Carolina, from the British. Hawkins fought at the Battle of Monmouth, a significant 1778 battle in New Jersey, and after the war was a founder of the Society of the Cincinnati, an organization composed of former Patriot leaders.[27] Bute County landowners served on the Halifax District Committee of Safety and attended the meeting of the provincial congress that drew up the famous Halifax Resolves (1776), an early document that supported independence. Back in the county, local participants played their own part. In a pact from the period, Bute County citizens pledged to "join [their] hearts and hands in embodying [themselves] into an independent company of free men" to protect the county against "the arbitrary and dispotick [*sic*] power of a corrupt ministry."[28] A 1778 act passed by the state General Assembly allocated 105 citizens from Bute County to the militia.[29] Citizens of the county fought in many of the war's most influential battles, including the Battles of Camden, Charlotte and Guilford Courthouse. Bute County's (and, later, Franklin County's) militia was called several times to muster at the courthouse; the most important of these calls came near the end of the war, when Lord Cornwallis marched through the area on his way to Yorktown.[30]

During the Revolution, many of Franklin County's eventual founders moved out of the shadows of their northern Bute neighbors. Benjamin Seawell, who had moved from southeast Virginia to Bute County in 1770, became a militia leader during the Revolution and served in the local committee of safety.[31] He became a colonel, corresponded with Sumner and advocated strongly on behalf of his troops. In a 1780 letter to future governor Abner Nash, Seawell requested higher pay for his men and wrote, "The men are fine men, full of spirits, exceedingly willing to march if they can only receive the bounty they were promised, and I flatter myself, under God, with doing much good if the troops can only be treated as the law points out."[32] Seawell was joined in his achievements by other southern Bute citizens, including Thomas Sherrod and Benjamin Person. Sherrod's family had lived in the area since 1760. He served as a justice of the peace in Bute County and led a local militia company as a colonel.[33] Several other members of the Person family were also prominent in the local militia. William Person signed a Bute County tax petition in 1775, a rebellious document in which the county's citizens argued, "We do absolutely believe that neither the Parliament of Great Britain nor any member or constituent branch thereof have a right to impose taxes upon these colonies to regulate the internal police thereof."[34] Person later represented the county in the Halifax Delegation of 1776.

Green Hill Jr. also represented the county at numerous national and state delegations during the Revolutionary period. Hill's family had lived in Granville, and then Bute County, for several decades; his father was a vestryman, and his brothers served as militiamen and political leaders. Shortly after the end of the Revolution, Hill's family received permission from the state government to build a gristmill on the Tar River. They also built the still-extant Green Hill House, a stately home with Georgian accents and fine wooden interior details.[35] Hill united two prominent southern Bute families in 1773, when he married Mary Seawell, the sister of Benjamin Seawell.

Although Hill fought in the Bute County Militia under Colonel Thomas Eaton, he was more of a religious leader than a military commander. In the decades before the Revolution, the county's religious character had mostly been defined by the Church of England. However, the hierarchical, state-supported church lost popularity during the Great Awakening, as traveling preachers brought new religious ideas from Europe and the rest of the colonies to the Piedmont region of North Carolina. Examples of this new religious approach could be found in the preachings of Henry Patillo, an influential Presbyterian minister who lived in Orange, Bute and, later, Granville Counties. Patillo helped establish a Presbyterian church in the area and served in the provincial congress. He also ran a Presbyterian school in Granville County for several decades, wrote tracts on religion and published a book of sermons. Outside of the Presbyterian population that reflected Patillo's influence, Bute County's residents were members of either the older Church of England or the Baptist Church, religious groups that also defined the rest of the North Carolina Piedmont region.

Green Hill Jr. helped add Methodism to that mix. While traveling preachers had already introduced Methodism to North Carolina (it was already particularly strong in Halifax County before the Revolution), Hill specifically brought the ideas of the denomination to Bute and Franklin Counties. Hill, who had converted to Methodism sometime in the 1770s, acted as a chaplain in the Revolutionary Army, and he began preaching in Franklin County after the war. As a prominent Methodist preacher, and as a political leader, Hill helped grow the Methodist congregation through his simple sermons and connections with other ministers.[36] Along with Jesse Lee and Edward Dromgoole, Hill was one of the most well-known and successful Methodist preachers on the Carolina Circuit, which comprised the entirety of the state and was formed in 1776.[37]

During the war, the movement to break up Bute County gained new momentum. The southern half of the county had grown in the previous decades; its plantations grew larger, with some of the largest landowners owning over sixty slaves. At the same time, the northern landowners had an incentive to keep the county as one. The state constitution of 1776 established the General Assembly, which comprised the state Senate and the House of Commons, and one state Senate seat was apportioned per county. A new county would mean that both the powerful landowners in the east and the prominent citizens of northern Bute County, who were gaining power in the state at a faster rate than the citizens in the southern half, would have less power in the state Senate. This power differential became clear as southern Bute County began to assert its rights and prerogatives during the first General Assembly session held under the new constitution.

In 1777, Bute County state senator Benjamin Seawell introduced a bill dividing the county in half at Shocco Creek. Seawell's bill did not mention the controversial name of the county but argued that "the large extent of the County of Bute renders the attendance of the inhabitants in the extreme parts of said county to do public duties extremely difficult and expensive."[38] That bill was read and passed by the Senate but went unread in the House of Commons. The bill failed again in the House of Commons in November 1777. According to residents of the southern half of the county, the delay was the result of the "erroneous representations that have been made by a few individuals, who for the sake of their own private care and convenience wish the county to continue undivided."[39] The residents from the northern half of the county were the most likely culprits of the slowing of the split of the county, as they stood to lose power in the General Assembly if the county was divided.

The bill that finally split Bute County was introduced in the General Assembly by Edward Jones, a House of Commons representative from the county's southern half, and it was passed on January 29, 1779. This bill ordered that Bute County be "divided into two distinct counties by a direct line from the Granville line to Halifax or Nash County line as the case may be," the dividing line being Shocco Creek.[40] The bill also ordered Bute County to be abolished—for the northern half to become Warren County and the southern half to become Franklin County. Bute County's old records were transferred to the new county seat of Warren

Green Hill House (late eighteenth century), site of the first annual conference of the Methodist Episcopal Church. *Courtesy of the Library of Congress.*

County. Jones's bill also ordered that the Franklin County court be held at a courthouse located on one hundred acres at the center of the new county. Until that courthouse could be built, the act provided for court to be held at the home of Benjamin Seawell.

A companion bill determined where that courthouse would be built. After surveying the area, the General Assembly purchased one hundred acres from Patewills and Jacobina Milner at the center of the county. On this land, the bill provided for the formation of a new town, named Louisburg (also spelled Lewisburg) after King Louis XVI, the monarch of France, America's closest ally. This town would contain the new courthouse, stocks and a jail. The legislature levied a tax on large estates and, for less wealthy citizens, a poll tax to recoup the money for the courthouse and the town.[41] Prominent Franklin County citizens, such as Osborne Jeffreys and William Hill, served as the first Louisburg city commissioners. William Christmas, the future surveyor of Raleigh and Warrenton, who was inspired by the designs of Savannah founder James Oglethorpe, was hired to lay out the new Franklin County seat.

Louisburg was an ideal location for the county seat for many reasons. It was close to many of the residents of the new county, as it was located only a few miles away from the Perry Plantation, the Green Hill Plantation and the lands of the Milner and Massey families. The site of the town had springs that provided an abundant water supply, and it was also located at a point where the Tar River could easily be crossed. To that effect, one of the few structures present in Louisburg at the point of its founding was Massey's Bridge over the Tar River, a legacy of the early Massey family.

While Bute County was ostensibly divided for reasons of convenience, the political context for the decision is clear. The two counties that Bute was divided into were both named for famous revolutionaries. Benjamin Franklin was a beloved American leader whose name appeared frequently in Revolutionary-era North Carolina writings and newspapers. Joseph Warren was a martyr for the Patriot cause, and he was the highest-ranking militia member killed at the Battle of Bunker Hill. As if to further excise the state's colonial past, in 1779, the legislature also split up Tryon County, another county named for a now-hated colonial official, and replaced it with Lincoln and Rutherford Counties, two more counties named after revolutionary heroes.

The late 1770s was a period in which Franklin County began to emerge from the shadow of its wealthier northern neighbor. It developed political leaders, a new center of Methodism and a town that became prosperous and well-known throughout the next century. The county began to diverge from its neighbor to the north, which it had been so closely connected to even before 1764. It is fitting that both the county and the county seat were named after heroes of the Revolution: the Revolution, in addition to creating a new nation, created Franklin County.

A TOBACCO COUNTY
IN A NEW NATION

1783–1839

At the nation's founding, the counties that had once comprised Bute County were on vastly different trajectories. Warren County, which was formed from the northern half of Bute County and named for Revolutionary War hero Joseph Warren, was on its way to becoming the wealthiest county in the state. It contained massive tobacco plantations and many of the finest homes that were built in the state before the Civil War. Two of the state's earliest governors, James Turner and William Hawkins, were born in the county, along with Nathaniel Macon, one of the antebellum era's greatest statesmen. The county's largest slaveholders in 1790, Herbert Haynes and Thomas Eaton, owned 138 slaves, and 10 other large plantation owners owned more than 50 slaves.[42]

On the other hand, Franklin County was in many ways a typical county in the new state. At the time of the 1790 census, Franklin County's population was 7,559, making it the twenty-first-largest county out of the fifty-four in the state; 2,717 slaves lived in the county, along with 804 heads of families and 37 people who were categorized as "all other free persons." Franklin County's largest slaveholder, Osborne Jeffreys, owned 69 slaves, and only one other slaveholder in the county owned more than 50 slaves.[43] A contemporaneous map of the state showed only one site of any kind, Louisburg, within the borders of the county.

The county's largest plantations had gained a modest amount of wealth over the previous three decades, which was reflected in the handful of fine homes located in the county. Several stately residences were built in the late eighteenth and early nineteenth centuries that survive to this day; these houses include Portridge (1780, near Louisburg)[44] and Monreath (late eighteenth century, north of Louisburg).[45] Two of the county's significant houses were associated with prominent women. The Patty Person Taylor House, a two-story late Georgian house with an ornate interior, was built around 1790 by Granville County politician Thomas Person for his sister, Patty. Patty, an heiress and wife of Louisburg Male Academy trustee Francis Taylor, lived in the house for the rest of her life. In nearby downtown Louisburg, Sarah Long Shine made her home, a quaint two-story house, at 303 North Main Street. Shine lived in the house for many of her eighty-six years, compounding homemade medicines and donating generously to Methodist education causes.[46]

Person Place occupies a unique role in the history of the eighteenth-century architecture in the county. It has both a Georgian wing, which was completed in 1789, and a Federal wing. The property itself is storied in Louisburg history, having been originally owned by early settlers, including William Massey and Patewills Milner. Matthew Dickinson once lived in the house in its early years. Jacob Mordecai, a member of the prominent Mordecai family in Raleigh, was also associated with the house for a time.[47] Wilson Milner, Patewills's son, built the original wing, while a later resident, William P. Williams, built the larger Federal section. The Georgian details on the southern wing of the house include a side gable, molded siding and a brick chimney with concave shoulders. The house served as a tavern for many years. According to local lore, Aaron Burr, former vice president of the United States and killer of Alexander Hamilton, was rumored to have once stayed at Person Place when it was a tavern.[48]

Another of the area's storied structures is Locust Grove, which is located in the northern part of the county. The extant Locust Grove is a two-story, five-bay home with a hall-and-parlor plan and fine Georgian accents throughout.[49] This house was built in 1790 by John Haywood, one of the most famous antebellum politicians in all of North Carolina. Haywood was the first mayor of the City of Raleigh, a lawyer and a state treasurer for over forty years. Locust Grove was his country home; Haywood Hall, another example of Georgian architecture, was his home in downtown Raleigh.

Most white citizens in Franklin County did not live in elaborate, sizable homes; instead, they lived in small log-built homes with one room, clapboard siding and shingle roofs.[50] While there is no remaining evidence of this, it can be assumed that Franklin County's free black people, such as Absolem Bebba and Benjamin Mabley, lived in similarly simple homes.[51] The county's

Person Place (oldest portion built in 1789). *Original photograph taken by the author.*

slaves often lived in smaller dwellings on the area's large plantations. Slave homes had dirt floors, no windows and often only one room. Most enslaved peoples' beds, furniture and tools were hand-me-downs given to them by their owners when they were no longer being used. In households with only one or two slaves, slaves slept on the floor by the fireplace.

Even with these modest beginnings, Franklin County soon had a large impact in many different areas—one of these was Methodism. Green Hill Jr., who brought the denomination to Franklin County, remained active in the Methodist Church after the Revolutionary War. During that time period, American Methodist leaders began deliberating on how to formally separate the church from the Church of England. They took action in the Christmas Conference of 1784, which was held in Baltimore; at this conference, leaders Francis Asbury, Thomas Coke and others began to ordain Methodist ministers. Asbury had been a frequent guest at Green Hill's home and had preached numerous times at the Green Hill House to the citizens of Franklin County. In 1785, Asbury returned to Hill's house, along with Dr. Thomas Coke, the first Methodist bishop, and several other Methodist ministers. This meeting, which represented three states in the South and over nine thousand church members, became known as the first annual conference of the Methodist Episcopal Church. Hill later hosted four more Methodist conferences in the eighteenth century, and his house was a center for Asbury's preaching until the bishop's death in 1816.[52]

The prominence of Methodism in the county did not, however, preclude the spread of other Christian denominations. There was still a sizable Baptist contingent and remnants of the Church of England present in Franklin County. Early Baptist churches in the county included Portege Chapel, Maple Springs Baptist Church and Sandy Creek Church; there was also a Baptist church in the western part of the county, Popes Chapel.[53] Presbyterianism also had a presence in the county, and it followed the preaching of Henry Patillo. There was also an early interdenominational church known as Shiloh, as well as a number of religious social groups, such as the Baptist Flat Rock Female Missionary Society.

Education was another area in which Franklin County gained fame. In 1787, an act of the General Assembly was passed to establish Franklin Academy, one of the earliest chartered schools in the state. The law provided for taxation to support the new school and a board of trustees that included local leaders like John King, Benjamin Seawell and William Green.[54] The trustees eventually procured land in the northern area of Louisburg, on the east side of the town common, for the school building. Franklin Male Academy, as the school became known, received another charter in 1805 and opened its doors that year. Its first headmaster was Matthew Dickinson, a Connecticut tutor who was educated at Yale. Dickinson's involvement was a primary reason for the early success of Franklin Male Academy. The academy offered courses in writing, French, English grammar and philosophy along with the standard classical curriculum of Greek and Latin. In many ways, Franklin Male Academy's curriculum matched that of the nearby University of North Carolina at Chapel Hill. Franklin Male Academy even received some students who had left the state university after its monitorial scandal, a student revolt in opposition to the school's strict personal conduct rules.

Dickinson's academy gained statewide recognition. Local advertisements praised the school for its bustling activity and well-behaved students, and prominent North Carolinians spoke at the school's early commencement exercises. At the first semi-annual examination in 1805, John Haywood said that the students would soon be "called upon to practice and perfect those arts which alleviate the misfortunates of mankind, or which adorn and dignify their nature," and he pushed them to serve as the "conductors

Restored site of the Franklin Male Academy (1805). *Original photograph taken by the author.*

by which the sacred name of liberty and of science is to be transmitted to succeeding generations."[55] The prosperity and success of the Franklin Male Academy continued after Dickinson's retirement in 1808. His successor, Davis Mayhew, had been educated at Williams College in Massachusetts and continued Dickinson's standards and enrollment numbers.

The example of the Male Academy soon inspired the opening of a female academy in Louisburg, across the town common, in 1814. Led at first by

Harriet Partridge, a well-qualified teacher from Massachusetts, the female academy taught classes on natural philosophy, chemistry and history, as well as drawing and painting.[56] The male and female academies operated across the street from one another in northern Louisburg throughout the antebellum era.

Franklin Male Academy was remarkable for both its quality and its longevity, especially when compared with contemporary academies. The legislation that led to the formation of the Franklin Male Academy was just one of dozens of bills that established academies all throughout North Carolina. Many of these academies, including schools in Salisbury, Hillsborough and Richmond County, closed before 1865. Several of these academies later became public high schools or had their buildings used for other educational purposes. With the possible exception of Hertford Academy in Murfreesboro, only Franklin Male Academy was able to maintain such close connections to a present-day institution of post-secondary learning, Louisburg College. Although it mostly originated from the female academy, Louisburg College still claims it is directly descended from the male academy and lists 1787 as its establishment date on its official seal.[57]

In contrast to the county's educational and religious developments, the frontier nature of Franklin County was more evident in the political scene. Several of the county's earliest leaders during the Revolutionary era soon left the area after the war; this was partially due to the effects that tobacco had on the fertility of the county's soil. William Christmas, after serving in the state Senate for Franklin County and planning the city of Raleigh, moved to Williamson County, Tennessee, where he lived for the rest of his life. Benjamin Seawell moved to Lebanon, Tennessee, in 1790, remaining there until his death in 1821. Green Hill Jr. moved to Tennessee as well in 1796; he built a home near Nashville and lived there until his death in 1826. Several of the leaders who remained, including Osborne Jeffreys and Thomas Sherrod, led long and distinguished careers as trustees and town commissioners. William Brickell served as a lieutenant colonel in the state militia, while Thomas Brickell, who represented several counties throughout the 1780s, served on the council of state for Franklin County.[58] Green Hill Jr.'s son, Green Hill III, moved into his father's house and served as a trustee for both the Franklin Male and Franklin Female Academies. His brother Jordan Hill served as a state senator in the North Carolina General Assembly in the early 1800s.[59] At that time, Franklin County's members of the General Assembly included Archibald Davis, Thomas Lanier and Eppes Moody.[60]

But along with its success, the county had its share of controversy. In 1785, Franklin County justice of the peace Robert Norris was banned from serving in that position again due to his "misdemeanor of being in company with people playing cards on the Sabbath day…and in consequence also…that the said Robert Norris hath been guilty of being in partnership with a certain James Massey in playing cards with a negro slave."[61] Other Franklin County politicians were also barred from serving due to significant debts. Even John Haywood faced a significant amount of controversy after his death. On reviewing his accounts, the state found over $60,000 missing due to Haywood's habit of using public funds to pay for personal expenses. The state filed numerous claims against his estate to recoup the funds.[62]

These shortcomings did not prevent men from Franklin County gaining a role in national affairs. One of the most consequential events of the early 1800s, the Lewis and Clark Expedition, had a Franklin County connection. A prominent leader of the expedition's journey from Fort Mandan (in present-day North Dakota) to St. Louis was Richard Warfington of Louisburg. Warfington was praised for leading the party through a harsh winter and remaining on the journey even after his tenure in the army was completed. He led a group of boats down the Missouri River and kept track of the expedition's journals, botanical specimens and crew of previous mutineers. Two years after the end of the trip, William Clark sent a request to the secretary of war that Warfington receive an additional bonus due to "the cheerfulness with which he continued in the service after every obligation had ceased to exist, from the exposures, the fatigues, labour and dangers incident to that service, and above all, the fidelity with which he discharged this duty."[63]

Back home, the county's early days were defined by slow growth and gradual organization and development. By 1800, the county had an established Masonic lodge. There was a blacksmith in town, as well as merchants and skilled craftsmen; attorneys set up shop near the county courthouse, and some of the town's most prominent citizens in the eighteenth century, most notably John King, were ministers. The aforementioned John Haywood led a small law school within the county. An 1810 newspaper article reported that Louisburg contained "about twenty neat houses."[64] Outside of Louisburg, the county was almost entirely rural. There was a small inn located in the far eastern part of the county called Webs Inn, and it appeared on an 1808 map.[65] But the first county post office outside of Louisburg did not open until 1821.

Visitors to Franklin County in the 1800s and 1810s noted its quiet, somewhat barren nature. Edward Hooker, a graduate of Yale who visited Matthew Dickinson during the tenure of his headmastership, noted that the county's "old worn-out fields in abundance" presented a "dreary decaying aspect."[66] Another contemporary observer wrote, "Franklin is rather broken but not more so than to render it agreeable—the soil, except on the water courses, is thin and stony."[67] The county could not even build its public buildings promptly and required new taxes to be passed in the 1780s to facilitate the completion of the county courthouse and prison.[68]

Transportation in the county was hampered for many years as well. Poor navigation conditions on the Tar River limited trade with the eastern part of the state. A 1784 law for improving navigation on the Tar River did not even mention Franklin County; instead, it allowed the county court of Edgecombe County to determine the length of the Tar River to be cleared.[69] Regardless, many early citizens, including Matthew Dickinson, believed that the Tar River could be made navigable in Franklin County. They supported the formation of the Tar River Navigation Company in 1816, with local businessman Joel King as its first treasurer.[70] But throughout the company's brief existence, the clearing and improvements associated with it mainly aided transportation in Nash, Edgecombe and Pitt Counties.

As for Franklin, its citizens had to use the old Green's Path and the east–west Tarboro Road to take agricultural products to market.[71] A post road connected Louisburg with Warrenton and the burgeoning town of Halifax to the north. A toll bridge over the Tar River (built in 1794) and a bridge over Sandy Creek (built in 1810) also aided overland transportation, but the county's isolation from major eastern centers of trade prevented it from growing like neighboring Wake, Warren and Nash Counties.[72] A bill introduced in 1784, which would have built a road connecting Franklin County to New Bern, was rejected in the House of Commons.[73] In the 1820s, when North Carolina began proposing and building new plank roads, Franklin County was left off of eventual routes and maps.

One area of economic success for the county came from its abundant waterpower. Some of the earliest artisanal activity in the county happened at its gristmills. In the years after 1779, the county's colonial mills were supplemented by a wide variety of mills, including Sill's and Whitaker's Mills on Lynch Creek.[74] Perhaps the most famous of these early mills was the one built by Green Hill Jr. on the Tar River near his home and the center of Louisburg. Hill's Mill was well known due to its owner and central location, but it was also known for its longevity. The mill remained standing until a fire in the mid-twentieth century, and the ruins can still be seen in River Bend Park in downtown Louisburg.[75] Along with spinning wheels and a sizable number of stills, Hill's and other mills allowed the county's plantations to produce a number of products to sell at market, often in Petersburg or Halifax.

North Carolina underwent several changes in the first three decades after the Revolutionary War. One of the state's earliest political battles did not reach Franklin County. In the 1790s and 1800s, the state, like the nation as a whole, was torn between the Democratic-Republican and Federalist factions. In North Carolina, these factions feuded over state finances and the independence of the University of North Carolina. The feud grew so heated that one governor of North Carolina, Richard Dobbs Spaight, was killed in a duel after a hard-fought election. Throughout this period, Franklin County was firmly Democratic-Republican. It was represented for decades in Congress by Nathaniel Macon of Warren County, one of the most staunch and articulate leaders of the Democratic-Republican faction in the country.

Franklin County did clearly participate in two of these early conflicts. The War of 1812, which was, in many ways, a continuation of the Revolutionary War, had a number of connections to North Carolina. British ships captured Portsmouth and Ocracoke for a few days during the war, and they launched several raids on the coast. Naval leaders, such as Otway Burns, and infantry leaders, such as Benjamin Forsyth—both from North Carolina—achieved fame and success in the war.[76] Franklin County sent over 150 troops to the conflict. These troops were members of the county's wealthiest families and included a number of Perrys, Hills and Davises among them.[77]

Another conflict in which Franklin County played a role was the long-running dispute over state education and state-level spending as a whole. The supporters of a public-school system, including Archibald Debew Murphey and Governor David Stone, believed that state spending on schools and internal improvements would enrich the state and help it overcome its backwoods, frontier nature. Opponents argued that governments should prioritize thrift in all possible situations. These opponents, led by Nathaniel Macon and Governor James Turner, were often more powerful and held the upper hand throughout the 1810s and 1820s.[78]

While Franklin County never wavered from its electoral support of Macon in federal elections, one of its representatives did take a bold stance against Macon's position in the state legislature. Charles Applewhite Hill, a nephew of Green Hill Jr., introduced a bill in 1825 that provided public funding for schools.[79] It created a literary fund that set aside money to help indigent students pay for academic training. The fund reached over $2 million by 1839—a considerable amount for one of the poorest states in the Union at that time.

The most important event in the South during the early years of the Union was, of course, the invention of Eli Whitney's cotton gin in 1793. Its introduction opened up millions of acres to cash crop cultivation and eventually turned cotton into the South's largest commodity. A cotton culture of large plantations, aristocrats and imported finery sprung up from the Mississippi River and traveled to the southern counties of the North Carolina Piedmont region. But Franklin County was excluded from many of these changes in the early nineteenth century. The county was too far north to become a center for massive cotton plantations, and it was too far south to take advantage of the fertile tobacco soil in the Roanoke River Valley.

Despite these shortcomings, the county continued to grow during the early years of the Union. It gained a slice of territory, east of Mockison Swamp, from Wake County in the 1780s.[80] The county's population grew by approximately 2,600 persons between the 1790 and 1810 censuses.[81] It was not until two events in the 1830s, however, that Franklin County reached a level of unparalleled success and fully emerged from the shadow of its wealthy neighbor to the north.

4

PROSPERITY AND THE RAILROAD

1839–1861

In 1839, Franklin County was forever changed by the arrival of the Raleigh and Gaston Railroad. The Raleigh and Gaston was formed in 1835 as a counter to the Wilmington and Raleigh Railroad, which had recently changed its terminus to Weldon and soon became the Wilmington and Weldon. The Raleigh and Gaston was chartered to connect Raleigh by rail to the town of Gaston on the Roanoke River, where it would have rail connections to the larger towns of Petersburg and Richmond in Virginia.

Franklin County was located on the direct route between Raleigh and Gaston. During the rail line's planning stage, the organizers of the railroad asked landowner Shemuel Kearney, the grandson of the colonial-era settler of Franklin County, to run the railroad through his western Franklin County land. Kearney agreed, with the stipulation that a depot be built on his land, near the intersection of the railroad and a road from Hillsborough to Louisburg. The depot was one of only a handful located on the approximately eighty-five-mile-long railroad line, and it immediately attracted commercial attention.[82] A group of entrepreneurs bought a seventy-acre plot of land around the depot from Kearney in 1839 and started a number of businesses.[83] Their plot, originally known as Franklin Depot, was incorporated as the town of Franklinton in 1842. Franklinton quickly grew and became home to several new businesses, including the county's first hotel, the Franklinton Hotel, which opened in 1840.

The Raleigh and Gaston Railroad laid the groundwork for another nearby town. A smaller community, known as Pacific, grew up around another depot and was organized a few miles south of Franklin Depot in 1839. Pacific received a post office in 1848 but grew slowly afterwards. Pacific was not incorporated until 1875, and it was named Youngsville after local resident John Young.

It is hard to overestimate the impact that the railroad had on Franklin County's growth and development throughout the nineteenth century and beyond. The county had finally conquered the geographical isolation that had plagued its growth since the colonial era. Its vast agricultural wealth could now be transported to Virginia and the rest of North Carolina without using wagons or clearing the Tar River. The railroad also helped culturally connect the county with the rest of North Carolina and the country. It facilitated the distribution of newspapers, travel and the eventual arrival of the telegraph in the county, all of which helped bring the world's latest news and technological advancements to Franklin County.

The introduction of the railroad was not just a product of luck and the good fortune of being located between the city of Raleigh and the new town of Gaston; the county was also welcoming and accommodating to the railroad. Kearney's decision to sell his land to the railroad was not universally followed by the state's landowners. Many other towns across North Carolina did not embrace the railroad—to their own financial ruin. For instance, the town of Milton in Caswell County, a burgeoning center for tobacco and furniture since the eighteenth century, decided not to push for railroad access and went into a decline that continued for decades. A similar fate befell Warrenton when its town leaders decided to not allow the Raleigh and Gaston Railroad through the town. While Warrenton remained economically viable throughout the nineteenth century, it never regained its place as one of North Carolina's wealthiest towns after 1860. In fact, the town lost 38 percent of its population between the 1860 and 1870 censuses.

Another event of the 1830s altered the fortunes of Franklin County. In 1831, gold was discovered at what later became the Portis Gold Mine in the northeastern section of the county. Portis was part of what has been referred to as North Carolina's eastern gold belt. The mine led to the formation of a community that was mostly composed of prospectors and the businessmen who catered to them. As the experiences of other antebellum mining towns show, the community that surrounded Portis was most likely full of hardscrabble men who wasted much of the money they earned and built few permanent structures. In a 1937 article, historian Fletcher Green wrote that of all the gold towns that emerged in North Carolina prior to the Civil War, only Morganton survived into the twentieth century.[84]

Tobacco also gained greater prominence in the county in the 1830s. Franklin County farmers had always grown some tobacco, but it was often supplanted by corn and other staples. This trend shifted in 1830, when Nicholas Massenburg of Wake County built a plantation near Louisburg. Massenburg kept meticulous records of his agricultural activities, so his experiments with large-scale tobacco and cotton growing are well documented. In 1839, he took thirty thousand hills of tobacco and twenty-seven bales of cotton to market.[85] His introduction of large-scale tobacco growing prefaced the bright leaf tobacco revolution, which began in 1839, when a Caswell County slave named Stephen discovered the bright leaf curing process.[86]

The introduction of the Raleigh and Gaston Railroad and Massenburg, along with the discovery of gold, helped spur an economic explosion in Franklin County. After a population drop in the 1810s, Franklin County's population grew by over 30 percent between 1830 and 1860 to 14,107.[87] The county's slave population grew significantly as well. At the time of the 1860 census, Franklin County had 7,076 slaves; it had the eleventh-largest slave population of any county in the state, and it had the eleventh-highest proportion of slaves (52.2 percent).[88] This proportion was greater than any of the state's other cotton counties and many of its earlier-settled counties, such as Granville, Lenoir and New Hanover.[89]

Franklin County's plantations grew as well. At the time of the 1860 census, Franklin County had one landowner, Thomas Alston, who owned over one hundred slaves. Only eighty-six individuals in the state owned more than one hundred slaves, and the vast majority of these slave owners lived in counties east of Franklin County. Members of the Perry, McKnight and Yarborough families all owned over eighty slaves. The growth of slave ownership also led to the growth of the free African American community in the county. James Boon was a local carpenter who helped build Nicholas Massenburg's plantation house and once performed repair work on the Franklin County Courthouse.[90] One of the most famous free African Americans in the state, Thomas Blacknall, also lived in Franklin County; unlike many of the other poor free African Americans in North Carolina, Blacknall was a blacksmith who owned slaves and a significant amount of property. Blacknall was a minority even among his own group of slave-owning African Americans. While many slave-owning blacks, according to historian John Hope Franklin, were primarily focused on freeing their slaves and treating them humanely, Franklin wrote that others "were more interested in making their farms or carpenter-shops 'pay' than they were in treating their slaves humanely."[91]

These men often owned a number of slaves and were not active in buying and freeing other people on a regular basis. Blacknall belonged to this more capitalistic group, along with the famous carpenter Thomas Day.

As a result of this increased wealth, the county became remarkably more sophisticated, both in Louisburg and in a number of other rural areas. This growth was reflected by the new post offices that sprang up throughout the county; eighteen new post offices opened in Franklin County between 1830 and 1860. Several of these post offices were located outside of Louisburg and the path of the Raleigh and Gaston Railroad, in places like Halls Crossroads (southeast of Louisburg), Cedar Rock (in the northeast section of the county) and Hayesville (in the northwest corner of the county).[92] Several of these post offices were the predecessors of later towns that emerged after the Civil War.

Some of the new industries that sprang up after the 1830s were expansions of older economic methods. Around 1850, Jordan Jones bought a tract of land in northeastern Franklin County that included Perry's Mill at the confluence of Richland and Sandy Creeks. The mill was originally a sawmill, but it was soon expanded to include a gristmill. By 1860, the Jones complex, later known as Laurel Mill, was the second largest industrial center in the county, and it produced corn meal, lumber and flour. Laurel Mill eventually spawned a small community and later a cotton mill. The original two-story gristmill frame is still intact and can be seen off Laurel Mill Road in present-day Gupton.

The county also embraced new economic ventures. *Thomson's Mercantile Directory* of 1851–52 mentions nineteen different dry goods and hardware stores, along with several hotels.[93] The manufactures section of the 1860 census mentions industrial concerns, ranging from agricultural implements to carriage manufacturers, hats, boots, turpentine and three leatherworking shops. In the same year, the total value of goods manufactured in Franklin County was $158,202, which was greater than the comparable surrounding counties, including Warren ($156,687) and Halifax ($115,665).[94] In addition to manufacturing, a newspaper was started in the county in 1846. The *Louisburg Union* was joined by three more newspapers before the Civil War: the *North Carolina Times* (1848), the *American Eagle* and the *Louisburg Weekly News* (both from the 1850s).

Economic success further spurred the growth of education, which had propelled Franklin County in earlier eras. Schools proliferated in the antebellum period; by 1850, the county had nine private schools, two academies and twenty-eight public schools teaching over one thousand

Laurel Mill (mid-nineteenth century), the last remaining site of what was once a much larger commercial complex. *Original photograph taken by the author.*

students.[95] These schools were well regarded and well represented in local newspapers. As a typical example, Hemdon Academy, near Louisburg, ran numerous advertisements in the *Raleigh Register* throughout the 1830s. An 1836 advertisement for the school reported, "Few neighborhoods are better suited for such a school. It has all the advantages of health, and good water, and good society. The people are industrious, moral and intelligent; and the undersigned feels assured that nothing like dissipation or idleness would be encouraged."[96] In the case of Franklin Male and Franklin Female Academies, the futures of the schools began to diverge in unique patterns. The Franklin Male Academy continued to operate in its 1805 building after the presidency of Davis Mayhew, but throughout the 1840s and 1850s, it was slowly supplanted by the growth of the Louisburg Female Academy across Main Street. In 1855, the previous decades of growth resulted in the Louisburg Female Academy receiving a charter from the state legislature to become a college. The all-female Louisburg College opened in 1857. The college held classes in a building that became known as Old Main; it was one of the largest structures in the county at the time, and it is an outstanding example of Greek Revival architecture. While there have been a number of additions to the building, Old Main is currently known for its expansive front lawn and towering Doric columns.[97]

As for religion, the Methodist and Baptist Churches still dominated the county. The 1860 census denoted eleven Methodist churches and twelve Baptist churches within the county. The county's new churches included Louisburg Baptist (1836), Ebenezer (1839) and Franklinton Methodist (1844), but a considerable number of other denominations were also represented. The 1860 census reported Presbyterian, Union and Christian church locations among several others within Franklin County.

Antebellum economic success led to a generous increase in the number of fine homes in the county. As tobacco continued to grow in importance throughout the county, a number of farm structures were built that survive to this day. Speed Farm was owned by Robert Speed, who bought the house from successful planter Archibald Taylor. Speed's farm often yielded over fifteen thousand pounds of tobacco annually, as well as smaller amounts of cotton, corn, wheat and hay.[98] To the south of Speed Farm lay Baker Farm; it is located near the Wake County border and mainly grew cotton and foodstuffs.[99] Several new houses in the county were designed by famed Greek Revival architect Jacob Holt. One of these was Vine Hill, the center of a plantation owned by Archibald D. Williams, a close relative of county leader Archibald Davis. Williams's plantation grew tobacco and cotton

Old Main (1857), the original site of Louisburg College. *Original photograph taken by the author.*

and was located in a prosperous northeast section of the county near the present-day community of Centerville. His home had the same hip roof and mix of Greek Revival and Italianate designs that defined all of Holt's buildings. Holt also designed the Archibald Taylor House (near present-day Wood) and the Samuel Perry House (near present-day Gupton), and he may have influenced the design of the well-preserved Williamson House in Louisburg. The Perry House is a striking example of Holt's surviving Franklin County work. Located at the end of a tree-lined lane near Sandy and Isinglass Creeks, the home is still in excellent condition. This house was owned for several decades by Dr. Samuel Perry, a descendant of the original Perry settlers who founded Cascine in the 1750s. Samuel Perry owned over three thousand acres next to his brother Joshua's even larger plantation. He lived in the house, ran his plantation and continued to practice medicine throughout the antebellum period and up until the 1890s.[100]

The death of Nathaniel Macon in 1837 was a sign of political change in the county on the federal level. Earlier, Macon had left the U.S. House of Representatives for the U.S. Senate, but the 1830s were a time in which

Williamson House (1850s), an architecturally significant antebellum house. *Original photograph taken by the author.*

Franklin County started to diverge from his influence and reflect on its recent political disputes. Throughout the state, the aforementioned Macon-Murphey dispute was replaced by a more formal party split between Whigs and Democrats. Democrats, following the populist influence of Macon, supported low government spending and free enterprise. On the other hand, Whigs fought for internal improvements and won support from the state's largest planters. Several North Carolina governors, including David Lowry Swain and John Motley Morehead, were elected from the Whig party in the antebellum period. As a consequence of its growth, Franklin County started to cultivate a considerable Whig following. In 1858, 372 voters chose the Whig candidate for governor, which was up from the low of 254 in 1838.[101]

The same local political names persisted throughout the antebellum period. The county's growth gave it two representatives in the North Carolina House of Commons after the constitutional convention of 1835. Numerous members of the county's largest families, including the Greens, Jeffrieses and Hawkinses, served in the House of Commons between 1835 and 1860. North Carolina's longtime state senators included John

D. Hawkins (1836–41) and James Collins (1848–55), while Guston Perry and Archibald H. Davis both served as local postmasters.[102] One unique political story from the antebellum period is that of William Jeffreys. In 1845, Jeffreys was a promising young state senator from the area of present-day Youngsville when he contracted a case of bilious fever. Delirious from the fever, he demanded that he be buried in rock so that his body could not be eaten by worms. When he succumbed to the fever, his father honored his wishes and buried him in a large rock near present-day Youngsville, off of Highway 401. While it has been vandalized repeatedly over the past 170 years, the tomb is still intact and can be seen today.[103]

Franklin County's political and economic success occurred at the same time that the nation was starting to split apart over the question of slavery. The Whig Party collapsed in the 1850s after it was unable to reconcile its Northern and Southern wings. Many of the nation's other institutions also began to break along sectional lines. North Carolina's representatives argued furiously on the side of the South during each one of the decade's crises, from the Compromise of 1850 and the Kansas-Nebraska Act to the notorious *Dred Scott* case. As one of the state's few majority-slave counties, Franklin County's growth in the nineteenth century placed it in the center of this debate.

One contributor to the nation's understanding of sectional differences was a onetime visitor to Franklin County. Frederick Law Olmsted

Jeffreys Tomb (1845), a curious tomb built inside a rock. *Courtesy of the State Archives of North Carolina.*

traveled down the Raleigh and Gaston Railroad in the 1850s, and in his book *A Journey in the Seaboard Slave States* (1857), Olmsted described Raleigh, Fayetteville and North Carolina in general. He noted that the state had a "proverbial reputation for the ignorance and torpidity of her people; being, in this respect, at the head of the slave states." He also said that this status came from the state's rural nature and the paucity of its eastern soil.[104] While North Carolina, including Franklin County, was not as dominated by slavery as many of the other Southern states, Olmsted still believed that it held the state back, writing, "One is forced often to question…whether humanity and the accumulation of wealth, the prosperity of the master, and the happiness and improvement of the subject, are not in some degree incompatible."

The conflict over slavery was often related to the lived experience of the South's slaves. In Franklin County, several of these experiences were captured by the Federal Writers' Project in the 1930s. The writers interviewed at least six former slaves, who had lived in Franklin County prior to the Civil War.[105] One of these narratives, that of Mary Anderson, was overwhelmingly positive. Anderson was one of many slaves who lived on Sam Brodie's plantation in Franklinton. She described her childhood as one of "good food, plenty of warm homemade clothes and comfortable houses," and she recalled several instances in which her owners brought her extra food and made sure she was well. She did not remember any corporal punishments: "[Brodie] had four white overseers, but they were not allowed to whip a slave…he didn't believe in whipping, so when a slave got so bad he could not manage him, he sold him." While Anderson mostly praised Brodie, she did mention that slaves were forbidden to read and write; she also discussed the frequent selling of slaves, which meant that families were certainly broken apart.

The rest of the Franklin County narratives did not reflect Anderson's rosy recollections. In her narrative, Lily Perry, a former slave of Justin Perry, who lived in Louisburg, described frequent beatings and the slave block in Louisburg, where she remembered witnessing women being torn apart from their young children. Ida Adkins described being forced to go hungry as a punishment, while Josephine Smith told of the grueling conditions of a slave mother sold from Louisburg and sent off to New Orleans.[106]

At least one citizen of Franklin County took a well-documented role in the fight against slavery. Daniel Reaves Goodloe was born in 1814 in Louisburg and was educated at Louisburg Male Academy. He later studied law and became a printer in Oxford, where he was first exposed to antislavery writings. Goodloe became one of the rare white Southern critics of slavery. He then moved to Washington, D.C., and worked as an editor and correspondent for the *New York Times*. Goodloe's 1846 work, *Inquiry into the Causes Which Have Retarded the Accumulation of Wealth and Increase of Population in the Southern States*, was a detailed and deliberate critique of slavery from a Southerner eleven years before Hinton Rowan Helper's *The Impending Crisis of the South*. In his writing, Goodloe took pains to compare the North and the South, arguing that slavery was the only factor preventing the South from becoming the wealthier section of the nation, as it had a larger population. He wrote:

> *Slavery affects the prosperity of the country by its tendency to degrade labor in the estimation of the poor, and to engender pride in the rich; and as a consequence, to produce idleness and inattention to business in all. And besides, it is said to have the effect of keeping away foreign immigrants, whose sentiments are averse to the institution. These combined causes, it is thought, have produced the great disparities between the North and South.[107]*

In 1860, the sectional conflict exploded. South Carolina seceded, fearing that the election of Abraham Lincoln would lead to the end of slavery; by the end of February 1861, six states followed suit, as they all shared South Carolina's fears. Virginia, Arkansas and Tennessee all seceded after Abraham Lincoln called for troops to put down the rebellion. North Carolina, which was surrounded by Confederate states at one point, became the last state to join the Confederacy on May 20, 1861. In a message to Lincoln, North Carolina governor John W. Ellis made the state's disgust with Lincoln's demand clear, writing that "the levy of troops made by the administration" was a "usurpation of power." He added, "You can get no troops from North Carolina."[108] The state seceded a little over a month later.

Franklin County was not an exceptional hotbed of sectional feeling, unlike Wilmington and the counties along the South Carolina border.[109] While it did vote for Southern presidential candidate John C. Breckenridge in 1860, none of the state's prominent fire-eaters represented Franklin County.[110] But like much of the rest of the state, and the South, Franklin County soon became a home of pro-Confederate sentiments and contributed more than its fair share of crops, materials and soldiers to the South's war effort.

5

WAR AND REBUILDING

1861–1877

At the beginning of 1861, in the span of a few short weeks, North Carolina went from a conflicted Unionist state to a full-fledged member of the Confederate States of America. In the weeks following the state's secession, Governor Ellis ordered the seizure of the federal arsenal in Fayetteville and the federal forts on the coast. The state began to organize munitions factories and supplies of food and materials; Ellis also asked for 30,000 volunteers and quickly organized ten regiments of soldiers.[111] These troops soon proved necessary, as North Carolina was an early target of the Union navy. Just four months after the beginning of the war, a contingent of over 2,700 Union troops captured Hatteras Inlet and established a starting point for the invasion of eastern North Carolina.[112]

Franklin County was part of the state's mobilization. At the very beginning of the war, several men, including R.P. James and E.A. Conn, left Franklin County in order to join the rapidly forming militia regiments in other counties.[113] Franklin County eventually organized a professional regiment of its own, the Forty-Seventh Regiment, along with men from Nash, Wake, Franklin, Granville and Alamance Counties. The regiment's members had connections to the most prosperous families in Franklin County. According to T.H. Pearce's list, there were approximately forty Perrys, fourteen Davises, fourteen Greens and six Kearneys who all served in the Forty-Seventh Regiment. The county's citizens also facilitated the critical usage of the Raleigh and Gaston Railroad to transport troops and supplies north to the war's eastern theater battlefields. In 1860, receipts from freight and passengers for the Raleigh and Gaston totaled $156,198. By 1863, that number had increased fivefold, to $817,615, and by 1864, it increased again, to $1,486,773. The railroad continued to be a lifeline for the Confederacy until the final weeks of the war.[114]

One of the most famous alleged contributions of Franklin County to the Confederacy—that of Orren Randolph Smith—occurred in early 1861. Smith was a native of Franklin County and a longtime army veteran, having served in the Mexican and Mormon Wars. In 1861, he responded to a call by the Confederate government in Montgomery to submit designs for a new national flag. Smith's design was one of the dozens that were sent in from all over the Confederacy, and it ended up resembling the eventual "stars and bars" design. While it is uncertain exactly how similar Smith's design was to the Confederacy's official flag, he declared that his design was the one that was chosen. But the Confederate committee on the flag and seal had rejected all submitted flags in favor of its own design.[115] But in the subsequent decades, Smith was regarded, along with Nicola Marschall of Alabama, as one of the two persons who most likely designed the first Confederate flag.

Troops from Franklin County were present at many of the Civil War's most decisive moments. Men from the county fought at early battles, including the Battles of Big Bethel and Hatteras. John Massenburg was one of the Franklin County soldiers killed at the Battle of Manassas, where Confederates scored a decisive victory over the Union army and protected the Confederate capital of Richmond, Virginia. After the Battle of Manassas, Franklin County citizens fought and died at pivotal battles, including the Battles of Malvern Hill, Bristol and Fredericksburg. There were also a number of local citizens who participated in the decisive Battle of Gettysburg, the massive Confederate defeat in 1863 that was a turning point in the war.

Franklin County civilians also played decisive roles during the later years of the war. One civilian gained a level of fame in the succeeding years: "Aunt" Abby House of Franklinton. Aunt Abby became known for her travels to the Confederate front lines in order to deliver supplies and tend to wounded soldiers. House also became famous for her bravery and her actions on the front lines of the Battle of Petersburg. She became familiar with Robert E. Lee, Jefferson Davis and North Carolina governor Zebulon Vance throughout the war and was described by Vance as "ubiquitous, indefatigable and inevitable."[116]

In 1864, North Carolina experienced a curious political event; the state held one of the war's few decisive state-level elections. Zebulon B. Vance,

Ellis's successor, faced off against William Woods Holden, a newspaper editor from Raleigh who ran on an explicit "peace platform." The county-level totals from this election served as an imperfect proxy for North Carolina's support of the war. While Vance soundly defeated Holden by more than 40,000 votes, a number of western counties, with a small number of slaves and a large number of Quakers, voted for Holden. Franklin County was firmly in the Vance camp, with 863 of its votes going to Vance and only 60 going to Holden. Several counties with large slave populations polled even more strongly for Vance. In the northeast corner of the state, Gates County, where slaves made up 48.3 percent of the population, returned just one vote for Holden in 1864.

The losses of the Confederacy at Gettysburg and Vicksburg, a decisive 1863 battle in the war's western theater, were simply too great to recover from, and the South lost considerable territory. Following the Emancipation Proclamation, many enslaved African Americans sought the freedom that awaited them behind Union lines. North Carolina's interior was invaded twice in 1865, once after the fall of Fort Fisher and again by General William T. Sherman's troops from South Carolina. The war ended in the state in 1865, when General Joseph Johnston surrendered his troops at Bennett Place, near present-day Durham. Johnston then marched to Greensboro, met with Jefferson Davis and disbanded the Confederate army.

Following the end of the war, Sherman's troops marched east, from Bennett Place to the eastern North Carolina railroads, and eventually to Washington, D.C.[117] On the way, a column of soldiers stopped for several weeks in Louisburg. Anna Long Thomas Fuller, a longtime Louisburg resident who lived on Main Street, dreaded their arrival. Upon Lee's surrender in April, she wrote, "I have not the language to depict the horrors of the past four or five days. The gloom and despondency that hang around everywhere is overwhelming. We are almost a conquered people; at least we are overpowered."[118] Once the Union troops arrived in Louisburg on May 1, Fuller wrote that they were "pitched in the college and male academy groves" and "behaved very orderly so far."[119] This appraisal did not last long, as six weeks later, Fuller wrote that the Yankees were "encamped in our beautiful college groves, which have always been the pride of the village and concentrated to learning, now polluted by the tread of the vindictive foe."[120]

The presence of troops in Franklin County was remembered differently by the slaves who were freed on their arrival. As soon as the troops arrived in Franklinton, Mary Anderson said, "Slaves were whooping and laughing and acting like they were crazy."[121] Mattie Curtis, another former slave who was interviewed by the Federal Writers' Project, described how the troops freed her from an abusive owner and how the army was followed by Northern preachers, who consecrated freed people's marriages.[122] Nearly all former slaves interviewed from Franklin County gave thanks to Abraham Lincoln for their freedom. A typical opinion on Lincoln was given by interviewee Hattie Rogers, who said, "I think slavery was an awful thing and that Abraham Lincoln was a good man because he set us free."[123]

The Civil War led to monumental changes in the South. One of the most immediate changes was the ascendancy of African Americans to positions of power for the first time. Northern leaders in Congress, who were later aided by President Ulysses S. Grant, sent federal troops to disenfranchise former Confederates and support the rights of recently freed slaves. The Thirteenth Amendment to the Constitution (1865) banned slavery, while the Fourteenth Amendment (1868) gave constitutional rights to the freed people, and the Fifteenth Amendment (1870) secured their right to vote. Troops were needed to protect these prospective voters, along with the many Northerners who had moved to the South to teach and organize the region's freed slaves. In North Carolina, African Americans secured the right to vote two years before the passage of the Fifteenth Amendment. They were given the right to vote by the state's constitution of 1868, which was adopted with the aid of black delegates.

As a county with an African American majority, Franklin County was at the heart of many of these shifts. The county boasted a large African American community, which quickly filled local and federal offices. One of Franklin County's most famous African American citizens was John H. Williamson, who moved from Georgia to Louisburg in 1858. Born into slavery and owned by members of the Perry family, Williamson learned how to read by the end of the Civil War, served as a delegate to the Freedmen's Convention of 1865 and gained his first government position in 1867, when he was appointed as a Franklin County registrar. Williamson was then elected to the state legislature in 1868, where he served for eight years in three nonconsecutive terms. In the legislature, Williamson strongly advocated for African Americans and their rights.[124] He introduced bills that proposed legal and social equality, and when those failed, he pushed for plans that would grant North Carolina's African American population land across the Mississippi River.[125] Outside of his time as a legislator, Williamson served as a justice of the peace and eventually as a newspaper editor in Raleigh. Both Williamson and James T. Harris, another African

American politician, served as delegates at the 1868 North Carolina Constitutional Convention.[126]

North Carolina's Reconstruction-era government also changed Franklin County's government and educational structure. The state's constitution of 1868 called for the remaking of local governments and the replacement of appointed justices of the peace with elected boards of county commissioners. These changes considerably increased the number of African Americans who served in local government in communities like Franklin County. There was also an expansion of schools for African Americans and the imposition of a school system that, according to historian James Leloudis, "promised, for the first time in the state's history, to educate all children, black and white alike."[127] Louisburg College, however, did not benefit from these changes. The college closed twice for brief periods after the war and was in dire financial straits; its experience was similar to those of many other Southern schools. The University of North Carolina, for instance, had invested much of its endowment in junk Confederate bonds, and it lost many of its students to both battle casualties and fear of Klan violence.[128] As a private college, Louisburg College was insulated from the politics of Reconstruction and suffered a slightly better fate than the University of North Carolina, which closed between 1870 and 1875.

At the same time, many white people in Franklin County suffered economic ruin. For those whose wealth was once held in land and slaves, emancipation led to their collapse. The construction of fine homes ground to a halt; the average value of farmland in the county dropped from eight dollars an acre in 1860 to only four dollars by 1870; and many families, like the Davises, lost their entire estates, as their money had been tied up entirely in Confederate bonds and slaves.[129] Aunt Abby House was forced to sell off her land in parcels and was eventually left destitute.

Certain aspects of life in Franklin County began to slowly recover, however. The county had new general stores and a new newspaper, the *Franklin Times*, which started publishing in 1875 as the *Franklin Courier* and continues printing today. Manufacturing was growing throughout the period as well, and agricultural failures, as well as the ever-growing Raleigh and Gaston Railroad, encouraged the growth of industry. The number of manufacturing establishments in Franklin County increased from twenty-two to twenty-six between the 1860 and 1870 censuses, and that number jumped to forty-six by 1880. The 1880 census still showed that flour and gristmill operations were the most significant manufacturing sectors in the county, with nineteen establishments employing thirty-eight people and creating $59,097 worth of products.[130] But it was during this period that Jordan Jones introduced the county to the textile industry when he opened its first cotton mill at Laurel Mill in 1869.

The county's civic institutions were also being rebuilt by two of its most prominent citizens. Judge Joseph J. Davis served in the Civil War and achieved the rank of captain before being wounded and captured at Gettysburg. He then ran a successful law practice after the war and was later elected to represent Franklin County in the U.S. Congress. Charles Mather Cooke was another politician and judge from the county; he helped reorganize the Louisburg Baptist Church and brought it the prosperity it needed to construct a majestic new church building in 1901.

The years of Reconstruction also encompassed the career of, arguably, Franklin County's most influential literary figure, Edwin Wiley Fuller. Fuller, the son of the aforementioned Anna Long Thomas Fuller and cotton broker Jones Fuller, attended the University of North Carolina in 1864, and he transferred to the University of Virginia after the war. When he returned to Louisburg, Fuller ran his father's business and became the mayor of Louisburg, all while furthering his literary career. Fuller continued to publish until his untimely death in 1876, at the age of twenty-eight.[131] Fuller's career comprised both verse and prose pieces. He started out as a poet, crafting such works as "The Village on the Tar" and "The Angel in the Cloud"; the latter, with its vivid imagery and sincere religious theme, won Fuller the most praise of all of his works. A contemporary issue of the *Franklin Courier* wrote that "Angel in the Cloud" showed "no mean handling of the poetic art, and in it are passages of genuine sublimity of conception and admirable expression."[132] Thirty years later, a compendium of literature in North Carolina went even further in its praise of Fuller, writing that "his work ["The Angel in the Cloud"] is regarded as the most original long poem ever produced in the state, and he is esteemed [North Carolina's] poet-philosopher."[133] Fuller also wrote a number of insightful prose works. His 1873 novel, *Sea-Gift*, was an influential exploration of the University of North Carolina and its experience during the Civil War. Fuller's book dealt with Southern life in frank, unsparing terms, unlike many of his contemporaries. Several scenes and themes from *Sea-Gift* appeared again in later appraisals of the South written by authors such as Thomas Wolfe. Fuller's book was also popular among students of the University of North Carolina, where it became one of the influencing factors behind the secret Gimghoul Society.

Almost as soon as Reconstruction began, Southern whites pushed back against its progressive policies in a myriad of ways. One was through the system of violence and terror organized by paramilitary organizations like the Ku Klux Klan. The Klan attacked both African Americans and their white Republican supporters. They murdered a number of African Americans across North Carolina and even lynched state senator John Walter Stephens in Yanceyville. Franklin County appeared, time and again, in the fight against Reconstruction. A report on a state Senate debate from August 1868 mentioned an alleged attack on Republicans in the county.[134] A more significant conflict occurred in July 1869, when Republicans met in Louisburg to nominate Philemon Hawkins for a seat in the state Senate. There was apparently considerable drinking, shouting and threats that stopped just short of physical violence. A conservative paper carried one of those threats, stating that, had it not been for the sobering presence of conservative leader Joseph J. Davis, "the carcasses of Gen. Willie D. Jones and Gen. Phil. Hawkins [the county's Republican senators] would have graced the oaks which stand before the courthouse, for they would have been hung."[135]

The county's pushback against Reconstruction was evident in yet another extraordinary political event that involved William W. Holden. Holden, who was elected governor in 1868, had declared martial law and suspended the writ of habeas corpus in order to fight back against the Klan. His actions appeared unlawful to many conservatives in the state, so the General Assembly voted to impeach him in December 1870 for violating the state constitution. After a long and contentious trial, the state Senate removed Holden from office and barred him from holding another statewide office. Holden became the first governor to be impeached and removed in the history of the United States, and he remains one of only eight governors who were impeached and removed. The state senator from Franklin County at the time, Philemon Hawkins, voted to convict Holden on two charges (Articles V and VI) and acquit him of the other six.[136] Hawkins's mixed vote was not surprising, given the county's politically competitive status following the enfranchisement of African Americans. Franklin County was one of the most competitive counties in the state in gubernatorial elections, with Republicans winning in 1872 by only eighty-five votes and again in 1876 by fifty-one.[137]

In addition to violence and political attacks, conservatives also waged a constant propaganda campaign against their white and African American opponents. They accused the state's Republican leadership of profligate spending, rampant corruption and general lawlessness. Joseph Davis parroted many of these talking points when he spoke to a Louisburg crowd

Joseph Davis (1828–92), Civil War veteran, congressman and state supreme court justice. *Courtesy of the Library of Congress.*

in August 1868. He described the Republicans as ruling with "fraud" and "wickedness" and said that they frequently committed perjury and flouted the state constitution by protecting the rights of African Americans. A letter to the editor of the conservative *Tarboro Southerner* described the speech as "one of the most scathing, exhaustive and unanswerable speeches it has been our pleasure to hear during the campaign."[138] County native Aunt Abby House became a symbol of the conservative movement in North Carolina. Aunt Abby continued to consult with and give advice to conservative leaders, as she had done for the Confederates during the Civil War. In 1876, she appeared in a cartoon that was drawn by a Louisburg businessman, which symbolized Southern women and conservatives who were pleased by Zebulon Vance's return to the governor's mansion in the election of that year.[139]

Several self-inflicted wounds also led to the breakdown of Reconstruction in the state. On the federal level, Franklin County elected John Thomas Deweese to Congress in 1868. Deweese was a former Union soldier and one of the state's most radical Republicans. He supported federal occupation, the disenfranchisement of former Confederates and the arming of Southerners who had been loyal to the Union. However, Deweese's corruption was used to smear all Southern Republicans in later historical works.[140] He was suspected of having paid off several of his competitors for the House seat—two of whom were prominent African Americans. In 1870, near the end of an investigation into potential bribes paid for a recommendation to the naval academy, he resigned from the House. When confronted with the allegations, Deweese was conciliatory but still remarked, "Hundreds have done the same thing before and will do it again."[141]

By the early 1870s, the constant pushback of conservative Southern whites had begun to take its toll. The national Republican Party split in 1872, weakening its resolve to continue fighting campaigns against the Klan and supporting local politicians in the South. In 1876, the nation split again in one of its most contentious elections ever. Several states sent both Democratic and Republican electors for president, and Congress was left to decide which electors to seat and, therefore, which candidate would win. The two sides agreed on a compromise: the House would accept the disputed Republican delegates, while the incoming Republican administration agreed to remove federal troops from the South. In North Carolina, the state's conservatives had already become so dominant that only Democrats were able to represent the state in the 1876 presidential election. There was only a handful of Republican officeholders left in the state, with Democrats taking back the legislature in 1870 and the governorship in the 1876 election. The removal of federal troops doomed any chance the remaining Republicans had for making up lost ground.

Franklin County had a mixed experience during Reconstruction. While it was not burned or ravaged by the war, like much of the South, the county still had to endure the upheavals of emancipation and racial terrorism. The county's African American population ruled admirably during the 1860s; nevertheless, the county still had to undergo the shift away from slave labor and toward some level of industrialism (which the entire South underwent in the years after 1877). The county remained primarily rural for the rest of the century. But in the future, Franklin County reclaimed its prewar level of prosperity through industry (primarily associated with cotton and tobacco).

6

RECONCILIATION AND
NEW BEGINNINGS

1877–1900

I n the years after Reconstruction, North Carolina attempted to erase the legacy of that period and reinstate many of the institutions that had governed it prior to the Civil War. The state legislature was solidly Democratic, ruled by conservatives and former Confederates. These lawmakers enacted a new constitution in 1875 that repealed many of the liberal reforms from the Reconstruction period, such as increased school funding and the popular election of county government officials. The state choked public expenditures for schools, reintroduced appointed local officials and staunchly supported railroads and other businesses.[142] African Americans lost most of their political power, although several still held office. Franklin County elected one African American, John Williamson, to the state House of Representatives for the 1887 term. Nearby, one congressional district called the "Black Second" was represented by an African American for fourteen nonconsecutive years between 1875 and 1901.

Two events, one symbolic and the other more material, occurred soon after the end of Reconstruction and were directly related to Franklin County. One was the participation of Aunt Abby House in the state Democratic Party Convention, which was held in Raleigh in 1876. At this meeting, some delegates reported that Aunt Abby House, a distinguished guest of future governor Zebulon Vance and others, cast a vote on behalf of Clay County's absent representative. This vote is sometimes referred to as the first instance of women's suffrage in North Carolina. The other significant event was the formation of Vance County. In 1881, the state legislature decided to form a new county out of Granville, Warren and Franklin Counties. In this act, Franklin County lost 130 citizens and $70,122 worth of taxable property in its northwestern section to Vance County.[143] This formation was clearly tied to the political power of Democrats, since it packed the most African American (and consequently Republican) sections of the aforementioned counties into one new county. Both Vance County and Pamlico, an eastern county that was formed around the same time, were created to solidify conservative power. For this reason, Vance County's first nickname was "Zeb's Black Baby," a term used from the very beginning of the county's existence by none other than Zeb Vance himself.[144]

On the local level, the 1880s were a time of significant growth for Louisburg. One of the catalysts of this growth was the decision by the Raleigh and Gaston Railroad to run a spur to Louisburg in 1885. Louisburg had been considered as a site for a railroad connection since 1831, and an amendment to extend the Wilmington and Weldon Railroad to Louisburg had been defeated by the legislature in 1869.[145] But in 1883, funds were raised, and the spur was finally built soon afterwards. The rail line was immediately effective in facilitating trade, commerce and the development of new technology. For instance, the amount of cotton handled in Louisburg more than doubled in the two years after the completion of the spur.[146]

The county's connection to the railroad accelerated the arrival of new trades and businesses. An 1884 general business directory lists dozens of buildings in the town, which the directory asserts had a population of slightly over eight hundred citizens. The town had a wide variety of businesses, including general stores, saloons, jewelers and livery stables. There were also a handful of manufacturing gins that used water and mechanically advanced steam power. By the end of the century, the town also had a telegraph owned by the Louisburg Telegraph Company and a telephone line.[147]

Gray's 1882 map of Louisburg indicates this expansion. A visitor in 1869 described Louisburg as a quiet, "ancient" town that was "not so prosperous as it once was."[148] But Gray's map from just over a decade later shows a livelier town full of a wide variety of houses and businesses. It shows a number of sizable homes, such as the main houses of the Crenshaw and Carlyle estates, and it displays the sites of Joseph Davis's and Charles Cooke's law offices, which were across the street from one another on Main Street. Gray's map also shows the cotton gin on the Tar River and Z.T. Terrell's Board and Sale Stables.[149] In 1896, a visitor from the Raleigh *Gazette* described Louisburg as one "of the most thriving little towns in the state, according to her size, and she has some of the cleverest and best citizens there that you will find anywhere."[150]

Franklinton grew throughout the same period as well. The town benefited enormously from the continued growth of the Raleigh and Gaston Railroad. It contained a wide variety of manufacturers and businesses, including tanneries, liveries, shoemakers and blacksmiths, which were listed in the 1896 Branson's Business Directory. In 1886, one of the town's best-known landmarks, the Franklinton Depot, was constructed. This building was commissioned to handle the increased traffic from the recently completed Louisburg line. The Franklinton Depot, which is still standing, has a number of Gothic and Italianate design features, including king post ornaments and double-leaf paneled doors. This depot is one of the few surviving nineteenth-century depots in the state.[151]

At the time, the town was led by older families, like the Kearneys, and newer arrivals, including the Cheathams, who came from Oxford in nearby Granville County. One of the earliest references to the Cheathams can be found in an 1884 summary of the county that was created for the North Carolina State Exposition of that year. This report mentioned a Captain I.J. Cheatham living and growing wheat in Franklinton.[152] A twenty-year-old T.J. Cheatham ran the telegraph company in Louisburg, while C.B. Cheatham managed a tobacco factory, and R.G. Cheatham was listed as a farmer in the 1896 Branson's Business Directory.[153]

The postwar period saw an enormous growth in industry that greatly benefited Franklin County. Throughout the Piedmont region of North Carolina, businessmen established textile mills that spun local cotton, ran on powerful rivers and employed impoverished farm tenants. Many of the state's largest textile mills were in the western Piedmont region, in towns like Alamance, Gastonia and Concord. While its cotton output did not match that of the southern counties, Franklin County still produced a sizable amount of cotton, totaling over 8,443 bales per year, according to the 1880 census.[154] This production, along with the county's numerous waterways and railroad connections, made it an attractive location for textile mills.

In 1891, Samuel Vann took advantage of these factors, as he planned to build the county's first large cotton mill. Vann had been in the cotton industry for many years and had worked for a cotton commissioning company in Baltimore.[155] He used his prior knowledge, along with capital from his Franklin County land, to organize investment. Vann had thirty investors by 1895, enough to purchase a stretch of land in Franklinton on the Raleigh and Gaston Railroad. Vann's mill, which was called

Franklinton Depot (1886). *Original photograph taken by the author.*

the Sterling Cotton Mill, was completed in 1896. It was a large, stately mill, with the towers and muted brick decoration of the then-common Industrial Italianate style. The Sterling Cotton Mill produced cotton yarn for consumer and industrial uses, and it fostered a growing community that housed, fed and provided supplies for its employees. By 1899, over two hundred people worked in the mill and lived nearby.

The tobacco industry arrived in Franklin County around the same time. Earlier advances in brightleaf curing had expanded from Caswell County to all of North Carolina in the two decades after the Civil War. At the same time, industrial centers emerged in cities like Winston and Durham

Sterling Cotton Mill (opened in 1895), a center of industry in Franklinton for nearly a century. *Original photograph taken by the author.*

to process the new tobacco for the consumer market. Rolling factories, warehouses and other industrial facilities sprung up across eastern North Carolina to fuel this demand. Tobacco prizeries and markets in towns such as Louisburg played key roles in Franklin County's economic growth. The county was dotted with barns, where tobacco was stored and then hung and cured. The boom in tobacco production went hand-in-hand with the growth of sharecropping, a labor system that locked both white and

Youngsville History Museum, formerly the Grace Fellowship Church of God, completed in 1886. *Original photograph taken by the author.*

African American farmers in a state of debt, poverty and reliance on large landowners in the postwar decades.

Youngsville, which had originally been named Pacific during the antebellum period, also saw significant growth after Reconstruction due to tobacco. After serving as a depot, Youngsville expanded into a sizable town with numerous churches and businesses by the 1890s. In 1896, town leaders founded a tobacco market that was immediately successful. The town was surrounded by the productive tobacco fields of Franklin County as well as the areas of Wake and Vance Counties that produced a considerable amount of tobacco. Youngsville was the home of the second bank in the county, which opened around 1899.[156]

Several other new towns and communities also emerged in the latter decades of the nineteenth century. One such community was Centerville, which is located in the northeast section of the country and was so named because it was nearly equidistant from Louisburg, Littleton (in Halifax County) and Warrenton. Centerville received a post office in 1874, and the town had two physicians and two general stores by 1896.[157] The mills of Jordan Jones also gave rise to a short-lived community named Laurel, which contained a creamery, cotton mill and general store near the original gristmill.[158] Other nearby communities that gained post offices by the end of the nineteenth century included Royal, Oswego, Ingleside and Pilot.[159]

The county's new prosperity enabled the construction of a number of new churches. The value of all church property increased from $11,600 to $57,140 between the censuses of 1870 and 1890. Along with the aforementioned Louisburg Baptist Church, in 1900, the Louisburg United Methodist Church, with its imposing towers and detailed brick decorations, was built on North Main Street.[160] St. Paul's Episcopal Church in Louisburg was also built in the same year. Today, this church stands out because of its Gothic Revival design features, which include a rose window and row of pointed arches near the portal.

Two of the county's leaders during Reconstruction also held important state positions in the last two decades of the nineteenth century. Joseph J. Davis served three terms in the North Carolina House of Representatives and returned, full time, to Louisburg in 1881. He worked as a lawyer and frequently told stories of his time as a prisoner during the Civil War at public events. In 1887, he was appointed to fill a seat in the North Carolina Supreme Court, following the death of Thomas Samuel Ashe. Davis served on the Court until his death in 1892. Charles M. Cooke took a similar path; after several years of service as a state legislator, he was eventually appointed as North Carolina's secretary of state in 1895. Cooke served in this position with distinction before he was defeated in the election of 1896. Cooke then became a superior court judge and remained in that position for over a decade.

In the 1880s and 1890s, throughout the South, political offices were dominated by former Confederate veterans, who used their military prestige to attain political power, and Franklin County was no exception. The county's representatives, judges and mayors often had familiar surnames. In many ways, leadership in the county conformed to the old families. Greens, Macons and Davises represented Franklin County in the state House of Representatives in the 1880s and 1890s. And Perrys, Battles, Davises and Kings all represented the county in the state Senate during that same time. But new industry, along with the upheavals of Reconstruction, led to the prominence of new names in the county.

The Fords and the Allens were two of the most successful new families in the county in the decades following the Civil War. George W. Ford moved

Left: Oswego (post office established 1892), one of Franklin County's small communities. *Original photograph taken by the author.*

Below: Louisburg Baptist Church (1901–1904). *Original photograph taken by the author.*

from Pennsylvania to Louisburg in 1871 and started a successful brick manufacturing business. He was also a tobacco investor and the builder of many commercial buildings in Louisburg's downtown business district. The Allen family was descended from William H. Allen, whose six sons were active in the cotton business. Five of the Allen brothers owned stately homes on the same section of North Main Street in Louisburg.[161]

In 1894, citizens of Louisburg witnessed the last legal public hanging in North Carolina, in an event that became known as the Day the Black Rain Fell. This spectacle occurred as the result of a random, senseless murder. Two years before the hanging, Tom and Calvin Coley, who were both from the community of Wood, robbed and murdered a Jewish peddler from Virginia. They were quickly arrested and sentenced to death. Public hanging was rare by the 1890s, as most jurisdictions carried out executions behind prison walls and out of the public view. Nevertheless, the two men were hanged at the Franklin County Courthouse on July 13, 1894. The day gained its name from the legend that black rain (which is now speculated by scientists to have been caused by either dust from crowds or soot from fires) fell around the same time as the hangings.[162] This rain served as a symbol for the brutality of the day, and the event was the subject of a 1984 true crime book of the same name.

The post-Reconstruction period also saw enormous changes in education in Franklin County. The most important change was the one that was experienced by Louisburg College. The Franklin Male Academy thrived under the tutelage of its longest-serving president, Matthew S. Davis, who led the school from 1855 to 1880, but the female college suffered numerous setbacks in the 1880s. The citizens of Louisburg intervened time and again to rescue the college; Joseph Davis even purchased the land and leased it to the college beginning in 1883. Charles M. Cooke then bought the property from Davis for $1,650 in 1889.[163] In 1891, the college was again rescued by the philanthropic Duke family; Washington Duke, just one year after buying Trinity College (now Duke University) and moving it to Durham, purchased Louisburg College.[164] The Dukes did not intend to run Louisburg College as they ran Trinity, however. Their purchase set the stage for the takeover of the college by the United Methodist Church, of which the Dukes were devout members. This act gave the college financial stability and the ability to grow. The graduating class of 1900 was the largest the school had ever witnessed up to that point.[165]

One of Franklin County's most remarkable teachers also worked during this time period. Moses Hopkins was an African American schoolteacher;

he was born into slavery in Virginia and arrived in Franklinton after graduating from seminary in New York in 1877. Hopkins founded Albion Academy, the county's first African American school, in Franklinton in 1879.[166] Albion grew considerably with Hopkins at its head, and it became one of the state's few normal schools for African Americans in 1885.[167] A 1902 book on African Americans in North Carolina described Albion as a school of good quality that prepared students for prominent historically black universities, such as Fisk in Nashville and Howard in Washington, D.C. Hopkins continued to cultivate his political connections

REV. MOSES HOPKINS,
OF NORTH CAROLINA,
NEW MINISTER TO LIBERIA.

REV. MOSES AARON HOPKINS.
A Sketch of the Life of the Man Upon Whom President Cleveland has Conferred the Important Diplomatic Appointment of Minister to Liberia.

Moses A. Hopkins (1846–1886), an educator and, later, an ambassador to Liberia. *Courtesy of ohiohistory.org.*

while running Albion. Unlike most African American leaders in the 1880s, Hopkins was a Democrat and was close to Democratic political leaders. When Democrat Grover Cleveland was elected president in 1884, Hopkins applied for a diplomatic post. The Cleveland administration appointed him minister to Liberia in 1885, where he served until his death, just a year later, on August 7, 1886.

In addition to three schools, African Americans in Franklin County also established a number of churches in the latter part of the nineteenth century. Mount Pleasant Presbyterian Church in Franklinton was founded by Hopkins and run by pastors who also taught at Albion Academy. Branson's Business Directory of 1896 notes that there were three churches for African Americans in Louisburg and two ministers resident. The county also had an African American newspaper, the *Freedman's Friend*, for a brief period in 1884.

Politically, the county was swept up in the late-nineteenth-century political movement known as populism. This movement was started within the Farmers' Alliances, a network of local farmer groups that came together to set up cooperative stores and pool together their resources. These alliances soon began advocating politically and formed into the Populist Party. Franklin County's farmers actively participated in this movement and began to organize Farmers' Alliances in 1887. In the same year, an article in the *Progressive Farmer* noted that organizers had started six sub-Alliances within Franklin County, in towns like Youngsville and communities like Flat Rock and Rock Springs. Organizers also established a countywide Farmers' Alliance in early 1888.[168] The boards of the county's sub-Alliances featured familiar county names, such as Young, King and Perry.

Franklin County's Farmers' Alliance was keenly interested in the development of common markets and improved agricultural techniques, but its members also followed and believed in the wider political implications of the movement. An 1889 resolution by the local Piney Grove Alliance from Louisburg illustrated this national focus perfectly; in it, the local alliance identified its enemy as "the moneyed conspirators of the United States," which were "combined against the farming interest to grind and extort from them their hard earnings; to enrich their already overflowing coffers." These moneyed interests "plainly [showed] in their thirst for gold that they [were extorting farmers], regardless of the misery and woe that they entail upon [the farmers and their] families." In order to fight these interests, the Franklin County Populists called for direct trade with Europe and the support of Southern manufacturers.[169]

In the 1890s, the county supported the Populist Party, which worked alongside African Americans in the state in a remarkable political process known as fusionism. The mostly black Republicans and mostly white Populists, working together, captured the state legislature and a vast majority of the federal House seats in the elections of 1894 and 1896, as well as the governorship in 1896. Franklin County also elected Populists to the U.S. House of Representatives and supported Fusionists over the conservative candidate in the 1896 election for governor.[170] The county also voted for a Republican (J.F. Mitchell) and a Populist (John T. Sharpe) for the state Senate in 1896 and for a Populist (Carter Barrow) for the state House of Representatives in the same year.[171]

In the late 1890s, the state's conservatives responded to Populism and Fusionism with an all-out racist attack. In the state's newspapers, they accused Republicans and Populists of fostering "negro rule" and threatening white womanhood. Democratic Party leaders openly endorsed attacks on black voters and ballot box stuffing. Officials in Wilmington supported a violent coup that overthrew the city's biracial city council. The attack killed dozens of African American citizens and led to a popularly elected government being overthrown for the first and only time in American history.

The coup in Wilmington signaled the beginning of the end of Populist rule in North Carolina. Conservatives triumphed in the state legislature elections of 1898 and 1900. A Democratic gubernatorial candidate, Charles Brantley

Aycock, ran on an avowedly white supremacist platform and supported a constitutional amendment that disenfranchised the vast majority of African Americans in the state. The amendment authorized poll taxes and literacy tests that excluded many African Americans, as well as poor whites, from voter rolls. This disenfranchisement occurred around the same time as the passage of dozens of laws that segregated schools, the militia and other public accommodations.[172]

Franklin County was an example of how the state turned so quickly from Fusionism to conservatism and white supremacy. In 1900, after years of voting Populist, the county voted by a margin of 1,200 for Democratic candidate Edward W. Pou, a law partner of the notorious white supremacy leader Furnifold Simmons.[173] The county also voted for the white supremacist constitutional amendment by a 1,000-vote margin.[174] In March 1900, an editorial piece from Louisburg supported the amendment; the writer argued that the amendment showed "the intention of the white people to control the affairs of state." He believed that "negro office-holding, in the South at least, [had] been a failure and [had] done the negro race more harm than it has ever done good." The editorialist predicted that the African Americans disenfranchised by the amendment would eventually see it as beneficial: "In less than five years, [the state's African Americans] will find that the adoption of the amendment will rebound to their good."[175] By 1899, the Jim Crow system of racial segregation had begun in earnest in Franklin County. That year, local officials passed an ordinance segregating Franklinton schools by race, and Louisburg created a rule that provided separate voter registration guidelines.[176]

By 1900, Franklin County was well positioned for the growth and success that awaited it in the twentieth century. In the census of that year, the county had 25,116 residents and produced $383,837 worth of manufactured goods—its highest totals ever for both categories. But just as industry and development brought continued prosperity to the county, the emergence of Jim Crow discrimination showed the county's white residents' unwillingness to equally share that prosperity for decades to come.

FRANKLIN COUNTY ASCENDANT

1900–1920

The early twentieth century was a time of contrasts for Louisburg; its earlier success, which was reflected in the growth of the town's business and the construction of its downtown commercial district, was threatened by the fire of 1905. During that event, several prominent businesses and homes were burned, including Cheatham's tobacco warehouse and houses owned by the Crenshaws and Fords. The fire caused over $60,000 worth of damage to the town's buildings and telegraph and telephone poles. As a result, the town recruited a considerable volunteer fire department, which had over thirty-five volunteers by 1908.[177]

The town quickly rebounded from the fire of 1905, as it was aided by national economic prosperity, high agricultural prices and the continued success of the railroad, which became known as the Seaboard Air Line Railroad in 1900. Many of the town's burned homes and businesses were rebuilt; the Crenshaw House was replaced by a domineering Classical Revival house that still stands on a hill on North Elm Street, overlooking the town. By 1910, there were a number of new businesses in Louisburg as well, including White's Furniture Company, the Louisburg Electric Company and Franklin Prudential, a building and loan association. Louisburg also had two banks by that year, along with a department store and a confectionery dealer.[178]

Near the end of the 1910s, Franklin County also became a site for new road construction following the introduction of the automobile in the early twentieth century. In 1916, the North Carolina State Highway Commission prepared a map of proposed highways. The map depicted several potential roads in the county, with one going through Franklinton and Youngsville and another going through Louisburg.[179] The county's business community responded accordingly; by 1916, Louisburg already had three car dealerships, which carried Fords, Maxwells and Dodges, and Franklinton had a garage for automobile repair.[180]

Louisburg's growth was reflected in the new homes that were constructed there during the early twentieth century, many of which reflected the grandeur and expansiveness of the Queen Anne style. One extant house from this period is the H.C. Taylor House, which was constructed in 1911 by the founder of a longstanding local hardware business.[181] Another is the George Murphy House, which was built between 1914 and 1922.[182]

Franklinton benefited in the 1900s and 1910s from its embrace of industry and its close proximity to Raleigh (via the railroad). The town's Sterling Cotton Mill thrived and continued to provide housing and wages to its employees in the community in order to fuel economic activity. By 1916, there was a washboard manufacturing plant in the town, as well as a printer and eighteen general merchants. The Kearneys and Cheathams worked in several important positions in the town, as did members of the Bullock and Pearce families, who served as mayor and town treasurer respectively.

Franklinton was also the site of new home construction. One prominent example of architecture from this era is the J.H. Harris House, which is located just a few short blocks from downtown. Harris, a local medical doctor and longtime resident, finished the building in 1904. The Harris House, a stately Queen Anne mansion that sports a tower and wraparound porch, is one of the largest and most ornate homes in Franklinton.[183] Other Franklinton homes from this time period include the Person-McGhee Farm (present appearance from the 1890s), the Aldridge H. Vann House (1918) and the C.L. and Bessie McGee House (1911), a large Arts and Crafts and Colonial Revival building on Mason Street downtown. W.L. McGee was a significant landowner and businessman who owned a tobacco warehouse in town. His son, Claude, enlisted an architect in Raleigh to build his eclectic house, which still has its original wallpaper and Arts and Crafts–style fireplace surround.[184]

The town of Youngsville continued to benefit from the growth of Wake County. It had Cheathams and Pearces in leadership positions as well, and by 1916, it had two manufacturing plants, a lumber plant and a bottling plant. However, Youngsville's main source of income was still tobacco. The town had two tobacco warehouses and five buyers, including representatives

Left: Person-McGhee Farm (present appearance dates back to the 1890s). *Original photograph taken by the author.*

Below: Vann House (1918). *Original photograph taken by the author.*

Opposite: Andrews-Moore House (circa 1790). *Original photograph taken by the author.*

from Liggett-Myers and American Tobacco, two large firms based in nearby Durham, in the early twentieth century. This number was impressive given that the town only had 431 residents recorded in the 1910 census.

While the cotton industry had aided the growth of Franklinton and tobacco had buoyed Youngsville, the county's plentiful forests led to the formation of the town of Bunn. A settlement had existed in the area around present-day Bunn since the eighteenth century; in 1792, William Andrews bought land eight miles northeast of Bunn and built what later became known as the Andrews-Moore House, a sizable two-and-a-half-story dwelling with Georgian, Federal and Greek Revival accents.[185] A church was also built there in 1788, and a large landowner named Green Bunn lived in the area. But the arrival of the logging industry and the subsequent extension of the railroad led to the growth of other businesses and the establishment of a post office in 1901.[186] By 1916, Bunn had a high school and a number of businesses, including a bank, a drugstore and five general merchants.[187] The census of 1920 recorded that 150 people lived in the town.

Despite the growth of these towns, the county was still overwhelmingly rural. As reported in the 1910 census, only 12 percent of the county lived in an incorporated town; more than 2,300 of the county's 24,692 citizens were rural tenants, and a large number of the county's other citizens owned their own farms. In the early twentieth century, farmers in Franklin County and elsewhere began diversifying their crops and growing more

foodstuffs than they had before. Tobacco and cotton were supplemented by grains, vegetables and fruits. While towns grew and high prices kept many farmers from starving, these rural tenants remained at the mercy of landowners and suffered frequent bankruptcies and foreclosures. This precarious nature led to an increase in farm sizes and the start of farm consolidation by the early 1920s.

The pace of growth in new rural communities, as shown by the number of new post offices, slowed a bit in the 1890s and early twentieth century. Only ten new post offices were established in the first decade of the twentieth century, as compared to the thirteen that were established in the 1880s. Several of these post offices were established in historically important parts of the county; for instance, a post office was opened in the community of Wood in 1900. Wood is located in the fertile northeastern section of the county, which had been prosperous ever since the eighteenth century. The community was located near Portis Gold Mine, as well as the large estates that once lined Shocco Creek on the county's northern border. The rural area near Wood began to decline, as the railroad bypassed it at first, but logging interests in the area eventually brought a spur and some economic development starting in the 1910s.[188] The railroad also originally bypassed the western community of Kearney, where the post office, which was established in 1903, was run by one of the state's few female postmasters, Lucy Kearney.

The early twentieth century was a particularly prosperous period for Louisburg College. The board of trustees of the college, which was controlled by the local conference of the Methodist Church, received official legal status by an act of the North Carolina General Assembly in 1909. A new structure, the Davis Building, was completed at the school in 1911, and it housed classrooms and the school's library.[189] Mrs. Mary Davis Allen served as the president of Louisburg Female College during this period. At the same time, teachers at the college were attempting to present a modern curriculum. Pupils studied basic fields, such as classical languages, English, history, physics and religion, but they also took courses in subjects that are less common today, including china painting and expression, a class that aimed to "directly stimulate the mental activity; to help to a realization of the creative powers of thinking and feeling; to lead to an appreciation of the best in literature and its portrayal; to train the natural languages of voice and body."[190] The school's catalog from 1919 noted that, while the college gave no degrees, "a diploma is given on the completion of the course of study required, which admits the student without examination to [the] best standard colleges."[191]

North Carolina's public education began to change considerably at this time. In 1901, Governor Charles Brantley Aycock launched an initiative to revolutionize the state's school system. As a result of his efforts, the state built hundreds of graded schools, increased teacher pay and ensured that more schools had libraries and textbooks. The state's white population in schools increased by 11 percent, and state funding of the segregated African American schools increased as well, although not by the same amount as it did for white schools. This trend affected Franklin County in a number of ways, starting with the historic Franklin Male Academy. The academy had been dwarfed by the female Louisburg College on the other side of Main Street, and it lost one of its most prominent leaders when Matthew Davis left the school in 1880. In 1905, the Franklin Male Academy was incorporated into a new graded school in Louisburg. Afterward, the academy's building eventually became the property of Louisburg College.

A number of other schools, both white and African American, opened in the county in the first two decades of the twentieth century. The county acquired three high schools, two of which were accredited by 1921. By 1916, the county comprised eighty schools, and at least nine of these schools were located in small, rural communities like Justice and Seven Paths.[192] One of the more prominent African American schools in the county was Franklinton Christian College, which was opened in Franklinton in 1891. Franklinton Christian College served up to 130 students by the early twentieth century, and it taught a wide variety of courses for men, women and children of all ages.[193]

Greater wealth meant that Franklin County could take advantage of the emerging forms of entertainment that characterized American life in the early twentieth century. By 1916, Franklin County had a number of connections to the world of mass media and culture. In addition to its department stores and institutions of higher learning, Louisburg also had a bookstore.[194] This store likely carried many of the books that were popular in early-twentieth-century North Carolina, including the epics of Lew Wallace and the dramas of William Dean Howells. The bookstore may have also had some of the new southern works of thought, like those by the critical novelist George Washington Cable and historian John Spencer Bassett, both of who wrote against the oppressive racial notions of their day.

By 1916, there was also a movie theater in Louisburg, which was known simply as the "Movies" in the *1916 North Carolina Year Book*. This theater played feature-length films as well as shorts, and it most likely displayed some of the blockbusters of the 1910s, including the famous but racist

Birth of a Nation. In the 1920s, going to the movies became a weekly outing for all classes, as everyone was eager to catch an epic or follow the next story in a Western serial.

Both Davises and Cookes filled various county leadership positions in the early twentieth century. A.B. Cooke was a local police chief in Franklinton. Edward Hill (E.H.) Davis served as a Methodist minister in Franklinton and later wrote extensively for the *Franklin Times.* His brother Marion Stuart Davis was a prominent architect. Members of the Davis family also served as postmaster generals and worked as blacksmiths, building contractors and cotton gin operators.[195] Fords and Allens also continued to be important to the economic and political life of the county. George W. Ford further expanded his real estate holdings, while James M. Allen served on the county's board of elections, and P.S. Allen (either Peter or Paul Allen) worked as a boot and shoe dealer and a clothier.[196] Many of the county's earliest families also retained influence as they navigated a more industrial and commercial Franklin County. The Yarboroughs, who had lived in Franklin County since the early nineteenth century, filled many important roles in the community. William H. Yarborough represented the county in the General Assembly in 1901, while other members of the Yarborough family worked as barbers and physicians.[197] Local boards and leadership positions were also still filled by numerous members of the Perry, Boddie, Person and Hill families.

One of the newest and most successful leaders in the county was lawyer Walter Bickett. Bickett was born in 1869 in Union County, North Carolina, and he attended both Wake Forest College and the University of North Carolina. He moved to Franklin County in 1895, married Louisburg native Fannie Yarborough and set up a successful law practice in Louisburg. Bickett was elected to the General Assembly in 1906 and gave such a rousing speech at the 1908 Democratic State Convention that he was soon nominated to be attorney general, a post he was elected to in 1908 and 1912.

In 1916, Bickett decided to run for governor. That year's election was the first in North Carolina to use the Democratic Party primary system. Bickett's opponent, E.L. Daughtridge, was a leading conservative in the state and had been a successful lieutenant governor in the previous administration. In the campaign against Daughtridge, citizens of Franklin County turned out to support Bickett. In *Bickett for Governor: The Record is the Reason*, the Bickett Club of Franklin County praised the attorney general for his sweeping oratory and diligent work ethic. The club collected a number of editorials that supported Bickett for their pamphlet, and in

Governor Thomas Walter Bickett (1869–1921), who resided in Franklin County for many years before being elected governor. *Courtesy of the Library of Congress.*

the foreword they stated their goal: "There is, to us, the promise of a statesmanship which understands, a character shaped and moulded by our own ideals, an ability proved in our service. We ask no more than that the state may know him as do his own."[198]

Governor Bickett came into the office with plans for an ambitious social program. Despite a recalcitrant General Assembly, he was able to enact several progressive policies during his four-year term. Bickett vastly increased funds for education, reorganized the state's taxation procedures and aided the state's fledgling highway commission. Bickett also expanded agricultural education programs and proposed reforms aimed at curbing the excesses of the crop lien system, which was a heavy burden on the tenant farmers in Franklin County and elsewhere. But Bickett's legacy was overshadowed by events that occurred four thousand miles away. The United States had been apprehensive about the current events in Europe, where an assassination in 1914 sparked an international war that led to over half a million casualties by 1915. But in early 1917, the renewal of submarine warfare and a proposed German-Mexican alliance was too much for President Woodrow Wilson and Congress to ignore. Congress declared war, and the United States allied itself with England, France and their other allies in April 1917. Over the next year, two million American troops headed across the Atlantic to fight in conflicts like the Battle of Chateau-Thierry and the Battle of the Meuse-Argonnes.

Governor Bickett heeded the call of war in the same manner as the nation's other governors; he supported the draft, advocated for the war and set up Liberty Loan drives. North Carolina contributed $110 million in Liberty Bonds and over $251 million to various charitable causes, including the Red Cross and the YMCA.[199] During Bickett's tenure, the federal government built a number of military camps in North Carolina, including Camp Greene and an internment camp for the crewmembers and passengers of German ships known as the Mountain Park Hotel. North Carolinians also worked diligently to support the war effort. Men and women donated items, volunteered with relief organizations and went without food and other necessities in order to bolster the troops. In a 1919 speech, Governor Bickett singled out the state's women for exceptional praise:

> *It would ill become the exalted dignity of their character to cheapen the women of the state with fulsome praise. Suffice it to say that once again they exemplified and glorified the genius of woman for sacrificial service. They gave their sons to the nation and to humanity, while their eyes flashed, and their hearts bled. They worked as hard as the men worked and prayed more.*[200]

The mobilization of the war effort affected Franklin County in much the same way as it affected the rest of the state; 795 Franklin County residents fought in World War I, including 320 African Americans, and 36 Franklin County servicemen died from either wounds or disease. [201] The war had other material effects on the county. In addition to irrevocably altering the lives of the families of the dead and wounded and creating a massive demand for agricultural products, the war also changed the men who traveled to the battlefields of France and Belgium. As W.J. Cash wrote in *The Mind of the South*, men from rural areas, such as Franklin County, experienced liberal, racial attitudes and learned ideas that were utterly unfamiliar to them. These men "had served for long months on the carrion fields of France—had stamped upon their shaken nerves for as long as they should live the macabre memory of interminable passage through a world of maggoted flesh, lice, mud, bedlam and the waiting expectancy of sudden death."[202] They returned to their rural homes with more fear than acceptance, and, in Cash's words, they were "filled with hate for whatever differed from themselves and their ancient pattern."[203]

The 1910s have often been referred to as the "nadir of race relations" in the United States. It was a time when African Americans in both the North and South suffered widespread violence and suppression. The North was wracked throughout the decade by a number of riots, which were partially due to the rising numbers of African American citizens arriving in the North from the South through the Great Migration. In the South, the white supremacy campaigns of the 1890s increased racial tensions and efforts to control and suppress African Americans, through either official policy or terrorism. An exhibition of this racial mindset was observed in Franklin County during the fervor over Louisburg's two Confederate monuments. The monuments represented both the county's commitment to its war dead and the ideal of white supremacy, which was reflected in the commemoration of a war fought to preserve slavery. One Confederate monument, depicting a soldier on top of a pedestal, was located near Louisburg College. This monument was dedicated in 1914 in an elaborate ceremony that featured a parade and remarks by then-governor Locke Craig.[204] In 1923, the United Daughters of the Confederacy erected the *First Confederate Flag* monument, a stone structure with carvings and segregated water fountains, in front of the Franklin County Courthouse. This monument was a result of the tireless efforts of Orren Randolph Smith's daughter, Jessica Randolph Smith, who spent years advocating for her father's official recognition as the designer of the first Confederate flag.[205]

Candidates in the early part of the twentieth century frequently appealed to white supremacy in Franklin County, and in other parts of the South, in order to win votes and castigate their opponents. In 1920, a typical embodiment of this mindset was printed in the *Franklin Times*. Under the headline "White People of Franklin County," the editorial ordered the white citizens of the county to "go to the polls and vote for white supremacy." This vote was necessary, the editorial went on to explain, since two northern Republican agitators had recently visited the county and "encouraged the negro to go into politics, told him he was good as white folks." Only by voting the straight Democratic ticket could white voters protect themselves, the African Americans under their charge and, most importantly, the county's white women.[206]

In addition to symbolic and electoral racism, African Americans in the county were also victims of physical violence during this period. Franklin County was the site of two lynchings in the 1910s. Walter Tyler was lynched in 1919 in Youngsville for the alleged rape of a white woman; he was taken from the constable who was holding him, killed and hanged from an oak tree near the woman's house. The *News and Observer* reported that, after Tyler's death, thousands witnessed his hanging, including his alleged victim's family and several African Americans in the town.[207] Later that same year, near Franklinton, Powell Green was murdered after shooting the owner of a movie theater. His body was dragged behind a car, hung and shot multiple times. This lynching provoked more of a reaction in Raleigh than Tyler's death. Governor Walter Bickett spoke out against the act in his home county the next day. He stated, "The members of that mob crucified the elementary principles of justice for which white men have fought and bled and died through a thousand years. They have assaulted the very citadel of our civilization and all the power of the state will be exerted to apprehend them and make them suffer the full penalty of the law."[208] Despite these harsh words, the perpetrators of Powell Green's murder were never apprehended. These events pushed many of the county's African Americans north in a process known as the Great Migration. The county's percentage of African Americans dropped from 46.8 percent in 1910 to 40.8 percent in 1930. This drop was slightly smaller than the one experienced in the state overall, which lost tens of thousands of African Americans to migration over the 1910s and 1920s.

But despite Jim Crow, several African American efforts prospered in the county. Albion Academy, along with Franklinton Christian College, continued to operate in Franklinton for several years under the leadership of J.A. Savage.[209] There were also many African American churches that operated in the county throughout the early twentieth century, including Old Phelps Chapel Baptist Church, Jones Chapel Missionary Baptist Church and Mount Pleasant Presbyterian Church.[210] While African American men were shut out of most factory jobs, many of them found jobs as artisans during this period, with six working as carpenters in Franklin County according to the 1900 census.

In 1921, shortly after leaving office, Governor Walter Bickett suffered a stroke and died at the age of fifty-two. He was buried in Louisburg's Oakwood Cemetery, among the many Davises, Perrys and Hills, whose families had founded the town but had never achieved the statewide success of this midlife transplant. Franklin County has not yet had another of its own residents ascend to the highest office in the state, but the period in which Bickett presided over the state was the culmination of two decades of significant prosperity. Franklin County was becoming an exemplar of industrial and agricultural success in the North Carolina Piedmont region, and in the following two decades, it was subject to the same forces of growth and catastrophe that convulsed the rest of the Piedmont region.

PROSPERITY AND CHALLENGE

1920–1945

The prosperity experienced in North Carolina in the 1920s was the culmination of the state's Good Roads movement. After years of private and limited public support, Governor Cameron Morrison signed a massive highway funding bill in 1921 and another in 1923. The amount spent on roads by the state government increased by $65 million through the bond proposals that resulted from these two laws. Morrison's road-building program helped farmers bring their goods to market and allowed factories to expand their customer and labor base. The road system helped propel the state's industries of tobacco, textiles and furniture manufacturing to the top of national statistics. It also aided in repairing the state's image and served as a source of pride. A 1926 travel pamphlet described the state's good roads as a selling point for visitors. The pamphlet's author wrote that, as a result of the new roads, "the interflow of the people has been multiplied, inter-sectional prejudices done away with, commercial life quickened and the minds of the people fixed on state policies, which can be initiated for and shared by the people as a whole."[211]

The state's new roads further connected Louisburg to the state's other economic centers; NC 56, which was completed in 1922, stretched from Franklinton to Louisburg and on east to Mapleville.[212] And NC Highway 561, which was built in 1925, connected Louisburg with Centerville and, later, Ahoskie.[213] But the first major highway directly between Louisburg and Raleigh was not built until 1932. U.S. 59 originally stretched between Raleigh and Warrenton; it received its current name, U.S. 401, in 1957.

The construction of new highways, along with a robust tobacco market, led to a host of benefits for Louisburg during the 1920s. Louisburg's population increased by 407 residents between 1910 and 1930. More residents meant the town had more demand for goods and a consequent rise in its business and industry. New buildings constructed in Louisburg in the 1920s included a new passenger station, a freight depot and a wide variety of auto parts shops and garages.[214] By 1923, according to that year's *North Carolina Year Book*, Louisburg was home to two national bank branches and one state bank branch, as well as eight practicing attorneys and three dentists.[215]

After Walter Bickett's death in 1921, the county's leadership mostly remained in the hands of its oldest families. Members of the Macon, Massenberg and King families all served as the county's General Assembly members in the 1920s.[216] There was one exception to this rule, however; tobacco magnate Willie Lee Lumpkin was elected to the General Assembly from Franklin County in 1928 and represented the county as an assemblyman throughout the 1930s, and he served as a state senator for several terms in the 1940s. His family was relatively new in the area, and they were recorded as living in Franklin County no earlier than the 1910 census.[217]

The county sesquicentennial in 1929 was an occasion for the county's leaders to appear in public and make a decisive case for the county's prominence. County leaders put on a sizable parade and invited a host of famous guests, including Congressman John H. Kerr, Albert R. Newsome and F.A. Olds.[218] Keynote speaker and former secretary of the navy Josephus Daniels gave a talk outlining the history of the county and lionizing its leaders during Reconstruction—many of whom he had personally known. The keynote speech was preceded by the singing of an "Ode to Franklin County" and was succeeded by a historical pageant comprising one hundred different characters from the previous 150 years of county history. The event was remembered in the *Franklin Times* as "one of the most glorious days in the long and interesting history of Franklin County."[219]

The 1920s also saw the emergence of Franklin County's first official historian, Dr. D.T. Smithwick, who was a remarkable man outside of the field of history. He was born in 1867 and began working as a dentist in Louisburg in 1896. With the proceeds from his successful practice, he was able to engage in other economic activities. The most ambitious of these side businesses was his attempt to revive the Portis Gold Mine, which he started with a land purchase in 1909.[220] His efforts were not successful over the long term, but he did become known in Louisburg as a learned man with an interest in history. In the 1920s, Albert

Newsome of the North Carolina Historical Commission established a county history program in which one person was designated as an official historian for each county; Dr. Smithwick was chosen to represent Franklin County.

Smithwick eventually worked his way up through the organization and served as the president of the North Carolina County Historians Society. As a historian, Smithwick did admirable work in researching the county's early history, and he collected numerous documents. He also wrote an early history of Franklin County's alleged role in the Tuscarora War and created a roster of local citizens who served in the Civil War. Smithwick also owned the home of Fenton Foster, an inventor who crafted an early practical typesetting apparatus that was one of the forerunners of the linotype machine. Smithwick's actions contributed to Foster's greater visibility in the twentieth century and his eventual reputation as an influential North Carolina inventor. While he never published a book of history, Smithwick served as a local authority, businessman and medical professional up until his death in 1956, at the age of eighty-nine.

E.H. Davis was another famed historian of Franklin County who operated around the same time as Dr. Smithwick. Davis, the son of Louisburg College president Matthew Davis and Green Hill Jr. descendant Louisa Hill Davis, was born in Louisburg in 1860.[221] He served as a Methodist minister for over forty years, both in Louisburg and at several other sites throughout North Carolina, including Goldsboro and Saint Paul. By 1915, Davis had returned to Louisburg, where he appeared in a Department of Public Instruction report as the principal of Louisburg High School.[222] After returning to his home county, Davis also began submitting historical sketches to the *Franklin Times*. He continued this practice for several decades, eventually publishing a book of his articles, titled *Historical Sketches of Franklin County*, in 1948. Davis's well-researched book was the first complete history of the county. It served as the definitive history of the county for three decades, and it is still cited today.

On the national level, Edward Pou remained the elected representative of Franklin County throughout the 1920s. Pou was one of the most powerful congressmen in the country; he served on the rules committee and on the ways and means committee throughout his tenure. Pou helped pass many of the core policies of Democratic presidents Woodrow Wilson and Franklin Roosevelt. Many of his electoral races only garnered token opposition, and at the time of his death in 1934, he was one of the longest-serving congressmen in North Carolina history. In many ways, Pou's legacy was similar to that of Franklin County's most influential legislator of the

Local historians E.H. Davis and D.T. Smithwick, circa 1948. *Courtesy of the State Archives of North Carolina.*

1920s and 1930s, the aforementioned Willie Lee Lumpkin. During the administration of Governor J.C.B. Ehringhaus (1933–37), Lumpkin became known for his support of greater taxation on business as opposed to a new sales tax. He was even suggested as a possible gubernatorial candidate in 1936, but Lumpkin did not end up running.[223]

The construction in the 1910s and 1920s of what would become U.S. 1 led to considerably more traffic and connections to Franklinton (U.S. 1 is a massive national highway that stretches from Key West to Maine).[224] The road bisected NC 56 at Franklinton and connected that town to cities as far-flung as Augusta, Georgia, and New Haven, Connecticut. Partially as a result of the new traffic patterns, Franklinton boomed in the 1920s. The town received a new bank, the Merchants Bank, during that period, and it had a capitalization of $50,000. Sterling Cotton Mill was bolstered by its success during the war years, when it made apparel and uniforms for the troops. Franklinton had a diversified economy outside of cotton. In 1923, the town had two banks, a hosiery mill, five physicians, numerous general merchants and a newspaper, the *Missionary Herald-Christian Star.*[225]

Another of Franklinton's most prominent buildings was also built during this time period. Franklinton Public School, now the Franklinton Middle School, was constructed in 1923 as a gift from Samuel C. Vann. At the time, it was built to replace an inadequate building that had been constructed only seventeen years before. Many cotton magnates around the state made similar gifts to local municipalities at the time, mostly in the context of building schools for company towns. Vann's school was not only a philanthropic gift for education; it was a statement in Franklinton, where it dwarfed most of the other buildings on Main Street. Franklinton Public School served the county's white population for four decades before integration. It is a sizable building, with seventeen bays and three stories, which was originally enough to house the area's elementary, middle and high school students. Today, the building is an imposing example of early-twentieth-century school architecture. It has numerous Neoclassical design elements, such as a row of pilasters and a flat pediment over the front door.

Youngsville experienced a different fate than Franklinton during that decade. Despite also being located on U.S. 1, Youngsville suffered a precipitous decline. The town's population dropped from 414 in 1920 to 395 in 1930. Businesses closed and economic growth slowed. A number of reasons have been given for this drop-off; T.H. Pearce argued that Youngsville was more convenient for travelers and businesses as a railroad hub than a stop on the highway, which meant that the town began to decline as automobile travel grew. Several of Youngsville's longtime business leaders died around the beginning of the 1920s as well.

Bunn, on the other hand, was mostly left out of the boom of the highways. As of 1936, there were no state or national highways running through the town. But its lumber industry persisted throughout the 1910s and 1920s,

Franklinton Public School (1924), one of the county's largest school buildings. *Original photograph taken by the author.*

fueled in part by North Carolina's booming furniture industry. Bunn's population increased by 62 percent between 1920 and 1930; the town had churches, an automobile mechanic and a railroad depot by the early 1920s as well. Although its commercial core survived, the town's growth slowed substantially after 1930, when the Montgomery Lumber Company ceased local operations.[226]

The 1920s and 1930s were a decisive period in the history of Louisburg College. Initially, the transfer to Methodist control and ownership was stabilizing for the formerly challenged school. The president of the college, Arthur Mohn, embarked on a building program in the 1920s, which led to an additional dormitory and a new structure known as the Franklin Building. But the 1930s once again presented issues of lower enrollment and stretched budgets. This general decline was exacerbated by fires in 1927 and 1928, which destroyed a number of buildings on campus, including the original Franklin Female Academy building. In 1931, the school made the momentous decision to become coeducational. This change opened the college up to hundreds of potential new students, and its enrollment grew accordingly. More students meant the school had more money for books, buildings, new teachers and new classes. The academy's course catalog of 1938 shows this considerable increase. In comparison with the academy's catalog from 1918, there was a wide variety of classes, including commercial law, child psychology and inorganic chemistry.[227] The college also boasted a professor with a PhD, mathematics professor Thomas Cicero Amick.[228]

One symbol of growth and modernization in Franklin County was the renovation of the county courthouse in 1936. Franklin County's existing brick courthouse had been built in 1850, with neoclassical detailing and a tower forming the main entrance. The renovation occurred after nearly a century of growth in the county. County officials hired a local, longtime architect, Marion Stuart Davis, to oversee the project. His courthouse was a traditional Greek Revival structure, with six Doric columns topped with a plain white pediment. The remodel removed almost all traces of the earlier structure and came at a considerable expenditure. Davis's austere building still stands in the heart of downtown Louisburg.

The 1920s were a time of lessening racial tensions in Franklin County and the country. After the riots of the 1910s, national organizations formed to advocate for African American civil rights and attempt to bridge the divide between the races. The most popular of these organizations were the Commissions on Interracial Cooperation, which first emerged in Atlanta in 1918. These commissions brought local white and African American leaders together to discourage violence and aid black schools. Another sign of this improved racial climate was the Rosenwald Fund. The fund, which

Franklin County Courthouse in Louisburg, North Carolina, on July 23, 1948. *Photograph by Clarence Griffin, General Negative Collection, Courtesy of the State Archives of North Carolina.*

was established by Sears Roebuck magnate Julius Rosenwald in 1917, built schools for African American students throughout the South in the 1920s. North Carolina had over seven hundred of these schools, and several were built in Franklin County. The Rosenwald Fund helped finance the first high school for African Americans in the county, the Franklin County Training School; the school's first class graduated in 1933. Money from the Rosenwald Fund also helped construct the Concord and Copeland-Perry school buildings, which are still standing today.[229] The Rosenwald Fund garnered widespread excitement from county residents, who donated as much as they could—even if it was only a dollar—to help provide the local funding match required to construct a school.

African Americans also built large, majestic churches in the county in the 1920s. One of the most significant of these was the First Baptist Church, now a part of the Louisburg Historic District.[230] This church, which was built in 1927, still houses one of the town's oldest African American congregations. It is a large brick building with castellations on top of a three-story tower. The front of the building displays a large round window and several stained-glass windows. Other churches built by the county's African American congregations during this period include Mount Pleasant Presbyterian Church (Franklinton) and Jones Chapel Missionary Baptist Church (between Ingleside and Centerville).[231]

Racial animosity did not disappear after the 1910s, however. Although lynchings decreased by more than 80 percent between 1918 and 1929, there were still at least five lynchings in North Carolina in the 1930s.[232] One of these originated in Franklin County. In 1935, murder suspect Govan Ward was abducted by a mob on his way to a jail in Nashville or Rocky Mount from Louisburg. The mob shot and hanged him, and his body was eventually found in Henderson. No one was ever arrested for the crime. The attack was one of the last three recorded lynchings in North Carolina, a state praised by W.J. Cash and others for its relative lack of lynchings when compared to other Southern states.[233]

In 1929, the shallow economic boom of the previous decade gave way to a massive bust. The collapse of the national stock market set in motion a chain of bank closures, layoffs and corporate bankruptcies. Farms went into foreclosure and businessmen faced ruin. The laissez-faire attitude of the state and national governments did little to aid average Americans, who were forced into bread lines and shanty towns. Rural families, like the vast majority of Franklin County citizens in 1930, were hit especially hard. The pages of the *Franklin Times* from this period are filled with foreclosure

First Baptist Church (1927), Louisburg. *Original photograph taken by the author.*

notices, many with familiar last names, such as Davis and Yarborough. Bunn's only bank, which was founded in 1915, failed during the early years of the Great Depression.[234]

Three years into the Great Depression, the American people elected a new president, who devoted himself to reversing the nation's woes. Franklin Roosevelt, who was elected in part by 4,294 voters from Franklin County, embarked on a program of bold experimentation in new government policies and spending proposals, starting with his inauguration in 1933.[235] Roosevelt transformed the nation's banking, securities and agricultural sectors. His relief programs provided millions of jobs and necessary services to people throughout the country. Despite North Carolina's conservative governance, the state's citizens benefited enormously from Roosevelt's programs, including the Works Progress Administration, the Tennessee Valley Authority and the Civilian Conservation Corps.

Franklin County received substantial assistance from the state and federal governments throughout the New Deal. The Works Progress Administration built the Louisburg Post Office on Main Street in 1937. This building is a standard example of New Deal architecture made of brick with stone accents. The foyer contains a mural, *Tobacco Auction*, that was painted by artists from the U.S. Department of the Treasury's Section of Fine Arts; it is one of dozens of murals depicting aspects of local life in North Carolina post offices.

Federal spending programs also brought improvements to the county's schools. The Public Works Administration built a school for African Americans in Centerville, the Perry School, in 1941. This school replaced an earlier structure that had been built by the Rosenwald Fund in 1928 and burned a decade later. The new school's layout was based on the Rosenwald Fund's Nashville Plan for schools as well as a design by Marion Stuart Davis, who designed several other brick schoolhouses throughout the county using funds from local taxpayers. The Perry School provided classes for eleven grades and served the county's African American students for over two decades. Along with this school, New Deal programs also helped build and remodel privies in schools across the county.[236] These improvements were made possible by the tireless efforts of longtime school superintendent E.L. Best, who administered the schools and applied for funds.

The programs of the New Deal brought much-needed support and infrastructure to the county. They were eventually combined with state programs under Governor Clyde Hoey, who took a bolder approach to fighting the Great Depression than his predecessor, Governor Ehringhaus. Franklin County benefited from Hoey's program to increase teacher pay and provide free textbooks to students. Hoey's successor, J. Melville Broughton, continued this program of education spending that brought badly needed funds to Franklin County.

The people of Franklin County tried to distract themselves from the Great Depression in a number of different ways. Some distracted themselves by supporting Louisburg's numerous sports teams. While the town had a particularly successful barnstorming baseball team in the early twentieth century, by the 1930s, the town's focus was on the Louisburg

Tobacco Auction (1939), by Richard Kenah. A New Deal post office mural in Louisburg. *Original photograph taken by the author.*

Perry School (first building completed in 1941). *Original photograph taken by the author.*

College team. In 1934, Louisburg College had its most successful season up to that point, winning sixteen out of seventeen games and beating foes such as the Duke University Freshmen and the team fielded by East Carolina Teachers College. In addition to baseball and men's basketball, the 1933–34 season also saw the fielding of a women's basketball team for a handful of games. According to the *Franklin Times*, the women's team made a great showing, despite considerable odds and no dedicated court: "Had they been able to play a full schedule, there is no doubt but what they would have been able to win several games for Louisburg. In all games, the locals played a very close game…at all times our girls played a clean sportsmanlike game that is much to be admired."[237]

Despite considerable federal intervention, the Great Depression did not fully end until the advent of World War II. In December 1941, after years of buildup and tension, the Japanese attacked the U.S. Naval base at Pearl Harbor. The U.S. Congress then declared war on Nazi Germany, Japan and Italy. This declaration was the beginning of massive preparations for war that dwarfed the sacrifices and scale of the preparations for World War I two decades earlier.

As in the 1910s, Franklin County answered the call for troops and supplies. "The fruits of victory will be shared by all and so should the sacrifices that precede victory," ran a *Franklin Times* editorial from 1942, summing up this ethos. Local citizens bought thousands of dollars' worth of war bonds, planted liberty gardens and sent massive quantities of food for the war effort. The day after war was declared, the Franklin County Board of Commissioners met and voted to postpone a plan to buy a new engine for the Louisburg depot, owing to the imminent need for steel in the war effort.[238] The next year, a massive scrap drive dominated the October 9, 1942 edition of the *Franklin Times*. One story on scrap noted that local schools had led in collecting scrap metal; in little over a week, the newspaper reported, "Franklin County has reported receipt of more than 50.000 lbs., although this is just the beginning of the movement."[239] The county lost fifty-two of its citizens in the fierce fighting of World War II.[240]

The war also created opportunities for women and African Americans. As in the rest of the country, many women in Franklin County filled the factory jobs that the drafted and deployed men had left behind. Women from the county also joined the Navy WAVES, the women's branch of the naval reserve.[241] These opportunities helped bring more women into the workforce—some for the first time—and helped set the stage for the drive for women's rights over the next two decades. A significant number of African

Americans also served in the war in segregated units. The experience of fighting for democracy abroad inspired African Americans in the county and throughout the state to wage a renewed push against segregation and the other precepts of Jim Crow.[242]

The period between the world wars was a twenty-seven-year stretch of fundamental shifts in the county. Between 1918 and 1945, Franklin County was reshaped as a result of highways and the Great Depression. Towns grew and faltered, depending on how they were connected to these new thoroughfares. The county's economy was blasted by the 1929 collapse, but many of its manufacturing establishments survived, and its vast agricultural wealth was able to be recovered with the help of government intervention. At the end of this period, World War II brought the county into prosperity, while it also introduced social changes that had profound effects over the following decades.

FRANKLIN COUNTY AND POSTWAR EXPANSION

1945–1979

North Carolina emerged from World War II in an unfamiliar position. It was becoming an economic powerhouse, driven by its three industries of tobacco, textiles and furniture. According to historian Hugh Lefler, North Carolina became the largest industrial state in the South by the end of the 1920s, a status that it retained throughout the postwar period.[243] The state was also modernizing far beyond the modest roads and schools of Cameron Morrison. In 1948, North Carolina elected a staunchly liberal governor, W. Kerr Scott, a straight-talking dairy farmer who appealed to the state's agricultural population and successfully took on the Democratic Party machine. Scott had a considerable impact on the state's economy and national status; his Go Forward program vastly expanded the state's spending and developed port facilities at Morehead City and Wilmington. Franklin County voted in favor of Scott in both 1948 primaries, with his total vote count surpassing that of conservative favorite Charles M. Johnson in the second Democratic primary by a three-to-one margin.[244] The county experienced the tumult of Scott's tenure and the postwar decades in a manner similar to the rest of the state.

In some ways, Franklin County shared in much of the postwar prosperity of the 1940s and 1950s. The county had representative sites for all three of North Carolina's prominent industries. Sterling Cotton Mill reached its sixtieth year of operations in 1955. It added a number of structures in the 1960s that increased factory floor space and production. The mill continued to provide jobs for a significant portion of Franklinton's population and contributed to North Carolina's continuing dominance of the nation's textile industry. Smaller businesses associated with the textile industry also operated in other county towns, such as Louisburg. The tobacco industry was represented by various factories and warehouses in the county. Franklin County farmers continued to produce tobacco, although the ongoing consolidation of farms drove more and more small farmers and tenants off of the land. While it operated at a smaller scale than textiles and tobacco, the furniture industry had a stake in the county as well. Both furniture and lumber operations were hiring in the county as late as 1964, even though one of the county's largest-ever furniture factories, the Macon Furniture Company, had closed in 1943.

For the most part, Franklin County's towns continued their patterns of growth from the interwar decades. Youngsville's population flattened after a considerable increase during the 1930s, matching the struggles of the tobacco industry and the town's earlier troubles. Louisburg and Franklinton grew significantly during the postwar decades, with Louisburg's population increasing by 27 percent between 1940 and 1970 and Franklinton's population increasing by 14 percent over the same period. One curious case in the county was that of Bunn. The town's population increased by 30 percent during the 1950s and dropped by 14 percent in the 1960s, even as the town modernized, with a new post office, new businesses and a new bank.[245] Even with its long-term growth, Bunn remained the smallest municipality in the county, its population topping out at 505 in 1980.

As in earlier boom times, entrepreneurs took advantage of the area's citizens' increased incomes and spending to open new businesses. One such business that survives to this day is City Lunch in Franklinton.[246] City Lunch was founded in 1949 by Clyde and Ruth Waiden on South Main Street. The establishment is one of the few remaining 1940s-era restaurants in the state, and it serves a traditional menu of hot dogs, hamburgers and homemade desserts. Many of these establishments, like the Roast Grill in Raleigh and Johnson's Drive-In in Siler City, are cherished by locals and travelers alike. They are often the subjects of profiles in media outlets like *Our State* magazine and the WRAL *Tar Heel Traveler* feature.

Another famed Franklin County restaurant, Sunrise Biscuit Kitchen, opened in Louisburg in 1978. Sunrise was founded by David Allen. The restaurant continues to serve homemade biscuits, sides and Southern staples out of its original location on Bickett Boulevard. The restaurant opened a second location in Chapel Hill in 1979, and it has become a staple of that town's restaurant scene. Sunrise has won numerous awards over the past

Left: City Lunch, a Franklinton institution since 1949. *Original photograph taken by the author.*

Below: Maria Parham Franklin (completed in 1951), originally the Franklin Memorial Hospital. *Original photograph taken by the author.*

four decades, including several awards for "Best Biscuit" in the *Triangle* and "Best Breakfast in North Carolina" in *Food Network Magazine*.[247]

A host of other consumer businesses opened up in Louisburg in the 1950s. Franklin County became home to a drive-in theater called the Car View Theatre prior to 1955, which made the county a part of the decade's national drive-in craze. There were also new department stores, auto mechanics, a radio station and grocery stores opened in the county.[248] Louisburg built its first modern hospital in the 1950s as well. The county took advantage of federal funds and a state program that was started with an initiative by Governor J. Melville Broughton in 1944. Local officials raised hospital funds from both higher levels of government and the general public in a years-long campaign.[249] Franklin Memorial Hospital, which opened in 1951, cost $500,000 to build and originally had fifty beds.[250]

Franklin County's position on a number of transportation routes led to a considerable increase in the number of immigrants to a provincial area, which had previously mainly consisted of African American, English and Scots-Irish families. The number of immigrants moving into North Carolina increased by over three thousand between 1900 and 1920; this was partially due to renewed opportunities in the area and the distribution of the massive influx of immigrants to the nation's northeastern cities from Southern and Eastern Europe.[251] Franklin County was not immune to this sizable growth. One of these immigrants later went on to obtain fame far from his home county.

Milton Supman was born in Franklinton in 1926, to one of the county's few Jewish families. He soon moved and joined the navy to fight in World War II. While abroad, Supman's penchant for humor and practical jokes led him to take on the comedic moniker of Soupy Sales. Sales ended up becoming one of the most famous comedians of the early postwar era. He became famous for popularizing the gag of comedians receiving a pie in the face; nearly every famous entertainer who appeared on his television show received one. While he gave frequent interviews and remained in the public eye for decades, Sales rarely mentioned his background or his hometown, but he once joked that Franklinton was so oblivious to the presence of Jews in the town that the Klan used to buy their sheets from his father.

Franklin County's postwar wealth allowed some of its citizens to take advantage of developments in technology and design. One example of this was the emergence of modernist architecture in Louisburg, in the manner practiced by Henry Kamphoefner and George Matsumoto at North Carolina State University. The most famous modernist house in Franklin County was the Dr. Thomas and Lois Wheless House, which was completed in 1955. The house was designed by G. Milton Small, one of the most prominent modernist architects in North Carolina and the designer of numerous homes and businesses throughout the Raleigh area. Small added elements from two famous architects, Ludwig Mies Van de Rohe and Frank Lloyd Wright, throughout the house, including a low-pitched roof, glass walls and an incorporated carport. The house remains one of the only modernist homes still standing in all of Louisburg, and it is the only Franklin County home associated with the architects who worked with Henry Kamphoefner at the North Carolina State School of Design.

But the presence of wealthy people and new businesses did not translate to general success for the county as a whole; much of Franklin County was still rural and poor. According to the North Carolina Bureau of Labor, Franklin County's average income per capita between 1962 and 1964 was $1,165, which ranked seventy-fourth in the state.[252] A state development plan issued in 1964 highlighted many of the reasons for this poverty and the county's general struggles. The plan argued that the county's population growth and

Thomas and Lois Wheless House (completed in 1955), designed by G. Milton Small. *Original photograph taken by the author.*

living standards had actually stagnated over the past two decades. It found that Louisburg's population increases had mostly come from new students attending Louisburg College. The hundreds who left the county in previous years—in a process known as outmigration—were mostly younger people who had left seeking more opportunities. Franklin County's towns and industries were simply too small and rural to meet the needs of many of its citizens, who wanted to pursue opportunities in the state's bustling cities. The plan eventually led to a new commission that was successful in bringing new businesses and industries to the county.

Franklin County received a new generation of leaders, who came of age in the years around World War II. None reached the statewide prominence of Willie Lee Lumpkin, who followed his prewar service with two more terms in the state Senate in 1945 and 1947. But several men represented the county ably in the General Assembly and various state and local offices. Wilbur Jolly was one of these leaders; born in 1916, Jolly served as a lawyer for decades in Louisburg, and he worked on a number of influential cases. He served three terms in the state Senate and one term in the state House of Representatives. Other well-known lawyers of this period included longtime representative Edward Yarborough and Charles Davis; both men were members of longtime legal families in Louisburg. In Franklinton, Henry Crawford Kearney, a member of the oldest family in the town, represented the county in the state legislature for one term in 1949.[253]

Outside of the legal profession and Franklinton, a number of men and women also left their mark on the county. Three women served on the Louisburg Town Council in the 1970s: Lois Wheless, Jane Saunders and Breattie C. O'Neal.[254] In 1970, Betsy Pernell gained a higher position of power, becoming the first woman to serve as Franklin County's commissioner. T.H. Pearce, a World War II veteran, became the unofficial county historian in the 1960s and published three books, including the comprehensive *Franklin County: 1779–1979* (1979). Cecil W. Robbins led Louisburg College throughout much of the same period and became one of the longest-tenured and most successful leaders in the college's history. In 1965, Louisburg College completed a sizable modernist library and named it after Robbins two years later.

One of the most prominent businessmen in the county during the postwar period ended up embarking on a significant political career. Clint Fuller, who was born in Vance County in 1920, was the longtime editor of the *Franklin Times*. As an editor, he won numerous awards for his investigative reporting and helped compile the paper's one hundredth anniversary issue in 1970.

Fuller also owned a supermarket and participated in local politics, eventually rising to the position of chairman of the Franklin County Democratic Party. But it was in his position as a newspaper editor that Fuller met Senator Jesse Helms. He soon became a communications director for Helms in 1973 and was promoted to administrative assistant in 1974. Fuller served in this position throughout most of Helms's tenure in office, retiring in 1991.[255]

The end of World War II helped intensify the movement for African American civil rights throughout the South. In two decades, a combination of direct action, court victories and legislative landmarks helped secure de jure protections for African Americans throughout the region. The movement is often seen as a set of major events, including the *Brown v. Board of Education of Topeka, Kansas* case, the Montgomery bus boycotts and the Greensboro lunch counter sit-ins, which eventually led to institutions being desegregated and African Americans winning specific rights and protections. But each event that made national news was often matched by hundreds of protests, lawsuits and confrontations on the local level. Civil rights were won as much in the courtrooms of Louisburg as they were on Capitol Hill and in the U.S. Supreme Court.

The most contentious and long-lasting fight for desegregation in Franklin County was conducted in the schools. The U.S. Supreme Court's *Brown* decision in 1954 required school desegregation but provided no enforcement mechanism, only a directive that the South's school districts follow its order "with all deliberate speed." Outside of high-profile cases, like that of the Little Rock Nine in Arkansas, most school districts did not start to integrate until the mid-1960s or later. In 1965, Franklin County began the long and arduous process of integration with a "freedom of choice" plan, in which a handful of African American students applied to attend white schools.[256] T.H. Pearce, a staunch supporter of segregation, responded by announcing the names of the children on the town's local radio station. Clint Fuller also published the names of the students in the *Franklin Times*. Soon afterward, the families of the children named by Pearce and Fuller suffered vehement attacks from local whites. Norine Arrington's family was awakened by rifle and shotgun fire into their home and car. Local white mobs fired at the home of Sandy Jones as well, while the family of Harold Coppedge was harassed by nails strewn in their driveway and a burned cross seventy-five yards away from their home. The local sheriff, who had recently attended a Ku Klux Klan open house, never found out who was responsible for the heinous attacks.

These actions had significant consequences. The U.S. Department of Education issued a directive banning the practice of announcing the names of integrating schoolchildren as a result of the Franklin County experience.[257] This directive also helped contribute to the debate over the freedom of choice plan, a debate that was waged vigorously between 1965 and 1968. Local luminaries, such as Wilbur Jolly and Charles Davis, aided Edward F. Yarborough in defending the school system. On the other side were a number of distinguished African Americans in the local area and beyond. Harold Coppedge's father, the Reverend Luther Coppedge, was one leading supporter of desegregation. A local pastor, Reverend Coppedge owned a twenty-acre tobacco and cotton farm, and his name was on the lawsuit pushing for prompt school integration.[258] Famed NAACP lawyer Julius Chambers represented Coppedge and the other plaintiffs in the case. The African American families brought the court case forward in December 1965 in the U.S. District Court for the Eastern District of North Carolina, and it was overseen by Judge Algernon Lee Butler. In early 1966, the U.S. Department of Justice (DOJ) intervened in the case on behalf of the plaintiffs. It was the first of these actions carried out by the DOJ, pursuant to the Civil Rights Act of 1964.

The acts of Pearce, Fuller and pro-segregationists in the county caused Judge Butler to lose his patience with the progress of the "freedom of choice" plan. In 1968, the judge agreed with the arguments of Chambers and Coppedge and issued an order that forced Franklin County schools to immediately integrate. School officials devised a plan and implemented desegregated classes for the fall 1968 term, with the help of FBI agents to prevent further harassment.[259] This decree was a seminal moment in the state's history of school desegregation, akin to the *Swann v. Mecklenburg County Schools* decision in 1969 that mandated busing nationally. The decree has been modified over the past fifty years, but it is still in force; it has helped keep Franklin County schools from segregating again to the degree that most other schools in the South have.

Along with Reverend Coppedge, Rosanell Eaton became another civil rights leader to emerge from Franklin County. Eaton was born in Louisburg in 1921 and cast her first ballot in 1942, easily passing the imposing literacy requirement that the county registrar had imposed to ban poor and minority voters. Through this act, Eaton became one of the first African Americans to vote in the county since Reconstruction. She worked tirelessly for over sixty years to register voters and advocate for voting rights. Eaton served as both a local poll worker and a special organizer to help register people. She registered over four thousand new voters during her time working for the state and the NAACP.

At the time, even the simple act of voting was a dangerous one and opened people up to ridicule and violent attacks. Eaton was targeted by local whites and the Klan, much like the Coppedge and Arrington families were around the issue of local school desegregation. But she continued her work and went largely unheralded for most of her life, until the 2010s. At the age of ninety-two, Eaton launched another campaign to fight restrictive voter ID laws in North Carolina. She became a lead plaintiff in what was eventually a successful case and was recognized in the *New York Times* by then-president Barack Obama for her long-running civil rights work. President Obama wrote, "I am where I am today only because men and women like Rosanell Eaton refused to accept anything less than a full measure of equality."[260]

The civil rights movement had an effect on the schools, businesses, political representation and social life in Franklin County. In an effort to fight desegregation and strengthen the power of white voters in North Carolina, the state legislature changed the congressional borders, affecting numerous counties. Franklin County was transferred into the second district, with Vance, Warren, Halifax and Northampton Counties, out of the much whiter fourth district. Its new representative turned out to be one of its most influential since Edward Pou.

L.H. Fountain, once a state legislator from Edgecombe County, was elected to represent the second district in 1952 and served in Congress for another thirty years. Fountain soon became a well-known congressman—one who led a number of committees and investigations on fraud and waste in government agencies. Fountain was also a strict conservative on issues of civil rights, particularly in his early career. After three years in Congress, he signed the Southern Manifesto, a pro-segregation document that advocated for a reversal of the *Brown* decision. Fountain often opposed the civil rights movement's initiatives that occurred in Franklin County throughout the 1960s.

The 1950s and 1960s produced significant changes in the state of North Carolina that later affected Franklin County. In 1956, Dwight D. Eisenhower passed the Federal-Aid Highway Act, which provided money from a gas tax to pay for the construction of massive highways throughout the nation. Several of these large highways, such as Interstates 95, 85 and 40, were constructed through North Carolina. The construction of interstate highways over the next few decades significantly changed the landscape of the state. Towns located along these highways grew immensely, as the thoroughfares provided easier access to markets for trucks and a boost in service industries that relied on car travelers.

Counties that were bypassed by the largest interstate highways, such as Franklin County, suffered accordingly, even though the county did gain some benefit from the paving of U.S. 64.

Politics and the high-tech industry also played a role in the eventual development of the county. In 1960, North Carolina elected another liberal governor, Terry Sanford, who viewed himself as continuing the tradition of Kerr Scott. Franklin County showed that its attachment to Kerr Scott was perhaps based more in his agricultural background than his liberal voting record, as its voters supported I. Beverly Lake over Sanford in 1960 by a considerable margin.[261] Lake was the clear conservative in the race, and he based his campaign partially on opposing integration and the example set by the Greensboro Sit-Ins.

Sanford transformed the state in many ways, from increasing the state's spending on education to combating rural poverty with the North Carolina Fund. But one of Sanford's most consequential decisions was the one he made to continue the work of his predecessor, Luther Hartwell Hodges, in expanding Research Triangle Park (RTP) in Wake and Durham Counties. RTP became a hub for technology in subsequent decades, and pharmaceutical, telephone infrastructure and computer companies opened and moved into the area—at first, slowly, then rapidly in the mid-1960s. This development helped reorient the state after its traditional industries and agricultural staples began declining in the postwar decades. The decline was slow but nonetheless evident by 1970, and it was initially due to international competition. RTP's growth, along with the growth of the finance industry in Charlotte, pointed an economic way forward for much of the state near these urban centers, including Franklin County.

In 1979, Franklin County celebrated its bicentennial. The event was marked by a fanfare similar to that of the sesquicentennial fifty years earlier. Louisburg was inundated with visitors, parade floats and decorations. Senator Jesse Helms spoke, along with Representative L.H. Fountain and State Representative James D. Speed. Local citizens worked on a number of historical projects that looked back at men and women who shaped the development of the county. With all of Franklin County's developments between 1929 and 1979—the changes in civil rights and technology being chief among them—many aspects of the county remained the same. While its workforce became integrated, Sterling Cotton Mill still produced apparel and dominated the Franklinton economy; U.S. 64 remained the dominant thoroughfare across the county; and thousands of citizens still worked in agriculture and the tobacco industry. But the developments in Raleigh and Charlotte, as well as the developments across the nation, radically transformed the future of the people of Franklin County.

NEW BEGINNINGS AND NEW CHALLENGES

1979–2020

In 1979, T.H. Pearce released his history of the county from the precolonial period to his present day. Near the end of this work, he made an appraisal of the county's recent history and its future. Pearce wrote, "Digging into the past, the accomplishments of those who preceded us here in Franklin County does make me proud, but then I feel that perhaps we passed our peak sometime in the late nineteen fifties or early sixties, and it is kind of depressing. I know that statement will bring accusations that I am pessimistic."[262] As evidence for this statement, Pearce brought up political corruption, recent debts taken to bring in new businesses and even the proliferation of "sexual freedom" and "venereal disease" in the county. It is perhaps no surprise, given Pearce's history during school desegregation, that his peak for the county occurred in the years immediately preceding the passage of the Civil Rights Act.

While his reasoning was biased, Pearce's appraisal of the success and decline of Franklin County was right in some respects. The county faced monumental challenges in the late 1970s and over the following four decades. The economic basis of the county was hollowed out, with many of the largest employers in the county turning off their machines and shutting their doors. The story of this decline is multifaceted, however, and it ends on an upbeat note, with the way the county has reinvented itself in the twenty-first century.

Many of the county's problems over the past four decades have been caused by statewide and national factors. Through the 1980s and 1990s, the state's three traditional industries started to collapse. International competition, trade policies and public health concerns weakened the state's tobacco industry. This decline was epitomized by the removal of the American Tobacco Company from Durham in 1987, which led to economic hardship in that city and the loss of hundreds of well-paying jobs. The textile industry experienced similar problems due to changes in trade laws and international competition. After many of the largest textile firms in the state merged and consolidated in the 1980s, the 1990s saw the closure of hundreds of firms and thousands of North Carolinians being thrown out of work. Many large furniture companies also collapsed, and there was a 56 percent decrease in total furniture manufacturing employment between 1992 and 2012.[263]

Franklin County was subject to these same forces. Many of the county's tobacco warehouses closed in the 1970s and 1980s. Tobacco production shrank, along with the production of other crops. The furniture industry, which had never held much of a presence in the county, shrank significantly as well (although a furniture plant did operate in Louisburg up until 2009).[264] The most disastrous closure in the county, however, was that of Sterling Cotton Mill, which shut down in 1991. The *Franklin Times* devoted much of its front page that day to a story on the closure and how it affected local workers. By that time, Sterling had become known as Franklinton Cotton Mill and employed 233 workers, almost all of whom were thrown off the job after their last shifts that cold January day. Wallace Summerlin, who had worked at the mill for thirty-seven years, was uncertain of what he would do next. "Franklinton is dying fast," he was quoted as saying to the *Franklin Times*. "Soon, it will be to where there just won't be anything left."[265]

The towns of Franklin County suffered accordingly. Louisburg lost 6 percent of its population during the 1980s; Youngsville, a longtime tobacco town, lost nearly 13 percent of its population during that same decade; and Bunn lost nearly a third of its population. Although Franklinton's population grew during this period, the town lost many of its largest employers. Many of the empty storefronts that now dot Main and Mason Streets in Franklinton were originally left vacant in the wake of the mill closings. Louisburg lost a number of downtown businesses as well. While employment in the town decreased for white citizens, it especially dropped for African Americans, who made up a large portion of the workforce in the town's tobacco and textile industries in the 1980s. Louisburg started to look like many Piedmont and eastern North Carolina towns that had become dilapidated by deindustrialization.[266]

Despite these challenges, Louisburg was able to make some progress during the 1980s and 1990s. One example of this progress was seen in the rise of Franklin County's most politically powerful woman. Lucy Allen, a member of the prominent Allen family, became mayor of Louisburg in 1980. She served as mayor for sixteen years, making her one of the longest-tenured mayors in the town's history. Allen also represented the county in the General Assembly for four terms (from 2003 to 2010) and served on the North Carolina Utilities Commission from 2010 to 2013.[267]

Franklin County's experiences and demographics helped shape its recent political history. It has voted for four Republicans in presidential elections since 2000, and it has voted for three Democratic governors in that same time period. It has been represented on the state level for the past two decades by an almost equal number of Democrats and Republicans. In 2019, the county had 16,497 registered Democrats and 12,744 registered Republicans.[268] There are a handful of reasons for this political makeup. The county has many rural whites who vote Republican, but it does not have the well-developed suburbs or wealthy areas that form the traditional bastions of Republican support in eastern states. The town has a high percentage of African Americans, who tend to vote Democratic. The county's rural status and middle-class average income have made it amenable to Democratic policies over the past several decades. However, its status in the 2012 and 2016 presidential races show that it should be considered the quintessential toss-up county.

Franklin County was able to remain a center for education during the 1980s and 1990s. Its public schools continued to grow and retained a diverse student body, as defined by the 1968 consent decree established by the federal court system. In higher education, Louisburg College achieved success as well. The stable, successful presidency of Cecil W. Robbins was succeeded by another competent administrator, Dr. J. Allen Norris Jr., who led the college from 1975 to 1992.[269] The college received its first female president since the 1910s in 1998, when Dr. Rosemary Gillett-Karam took charge. In 2010, Dr. Mark La Branche began one of the most successful presidencies of the past four decades, aiding the college through a massive recession and saving it from a threatened closure. According to *U.S. News and World Report*, Louisburg College's enrollment in the 2017–18 school year was 624. As of 2019, the school had eleven endowed funds, dozens of available scholarships and hundreds of classes offered each year. It had become one of the largest and most successful junior colleges in the state. The college's course catalog for 2019 explicitly stated the purpose of instruction at Louisburg College and most other junior colleges: "Dedicated faculty provides individual assistance, ensuring that each student is academically prepared to meet the requirements of four-year colleges and universities."[270]

The county also secured a significant educational investment when Vance-Granville Community College began offering classes in Louisburg in 1991.[271] Vance-Granville, part of the state's massive community college network, enrolled 3,329 students as of 2018.[272] This network helps prepare students for four-year programs and trade careers in cosmetology, auto repair, HVAC repair and many other fields. To that end, Vance-Granville's Louisburg campus has offered a wide variety of courses over the years, including British literature, legal research, salon and medical terminology.[273]

The process of deindustrialization occurred as growth in Wake County began to skyrocket. Research Triangle Park (RTP) started to take its place as one of the high-tech centers in the nation. Its earlier companies were joined by massively successful firms, like SAS, Nortel and GlaxoSmithKline. Factors, such as transportation, infrastructure and education, led to a growth in employment and subsequent growth in population. The expansion of RTP-associated towns was astronomical, with the town of Morrisville's population increasing by 1,802 percent between 1990 and 2010. But new employment opportunities and economic activity also led to a growth of bedroom communities surrounding the Triangle—some located in Franklin County. U.S. 1, like Interstate 40 and Six Forks Road, became a thoroughfare between residential areas and office parks where people work and shop. Growth extended north along U.S. 1, past Wake Forest and through to Youngsville.

The town of Youngsville has expanded immensely in the past thirty years. From the 1920s to the 1980s, the town's fortunes ebbed with the gradual decline of the local tobacco industry. But the growth of Raleigh and Wake Forest helped reverse that tide. Over the past three decades, the population of Youngsville has increased by 300 percent to its highest level ever, 1,293, according to a 2016 census estimate. The town's once-empty downtown area is now filled with businesses and restaurants. Numerous plants and companies operate within the town, including Amcor Rigid Plastics and Majestic Kitchen and Bath Creations. There are also dozens of businesses just outside the town limits on U.S. 1.

Raleigh's impact on Franklin County is clear when viewing the parallel development of Louisburg and Franklinton. Franklinton is approximately six miles north of Youngsville on U.S. 1; it has somewhat benefited from its proximity to Raleigh, with its population increasing notably over the past two decades. However, despite having nearly one thousand more people than Youngsville—and a more significant industrial history—Franklinton is currently struggling more economically. The mean household income in Franklinton is over $20,000—lower than the mean for the entire county.[274] Many of Franklinton's downtown storefronts remain empty and in disrepair.

Franklin County's role as a residential location has also been exemplified by a number of real estate developments that have opened in the past four decades. The largest and most significant of these has been Lake Royale, which is located on Cypress Creek, east of Bunn. This project was originally known as Lake Sagamore, a development proposed by a Tennessee firm in 1972.[275] The owners of Lake Sagamore quickly sold a number of plots and started construction before the lake was even finished. Soon, the project became an example of residential development going too far too fast, and the project went bankrupt in 1976. In 1978, National American Corporation bought the project (by then known as Lake Royale), and the lake was completed around the same time.[276] The community is now one of the largest census-designated places in the entire county. Its population of over 2,500 is exceeded only by Louisburg, and the community's median annual income is over $3,000 greater than that of the county at large. The gated community is unique, as it has its own police and fire department.[277] The community also has its own clubhouses, marinas and a restaurant that is open to the public. A 2018 study showed that there were over $2.2 billion worth of lake homes in the state and predicted that this number would increase.[278] Many of the prospective buyers of these homes live in the Triangle, and Lake Royale is half the distance from Raleigh that Lake Gaston is.

Like the rest of the country and much of the world, Franklin County was hit hard by the Great Recession that started in 2007. This multi-year economic catastrophe led to thousands of bankruptcies and the collapse of several of the country's largest banks. Subprime mortgage loans, which helped propagate and lead to the severity of the crisis, affected the county as much as any other part of the country. The county's unemployment rate hit a record high of 11.9 percent in 2010. Economic turmoil, combined with an anemic recovery, devastated many businesses that had survived or been opened after the height of deindustrialization. In quick succession, two restaurants opened and closed in a well-known red barn in Louisburg, partially due to the county's weak recovery.

In recent years, Louisburg has started to emerge from the disasters of industrial collapse and the subsequent Great Recession. Through this process, the town has started to form its own postindustrial identity.

An autumn day on Lake Royale. *Original photograph taken by the author.*

Dozens of new businesses have opened there since 2011. Bickett Boulevard in Louisburg is the site of new local and chain restaurants, as well as hardware and clothing stores. Downtown Louisburg also has a coffee shop, bookstore and local brewery. The town's River Bend Park has trails and playgrounds, and Louisburg College operates a botanical garden with trails south of downtown.

The status of African Americans in the town has also begun to improve. After being particularly devastated during the previous four decades, African American–owned businesses and majority-black neighborhoods have started to rebound. The town boasts one of the only African American–owned dentist partnerships in North Carolina, Hardy Smiles.[279] African Americans have played an increasingly important role in local politics. Sidney Dunston has served as a county commissioner for many years, some as chair; the same is true of Cedric K. Jones, the former agricultural extension agent. Dr. Elizabeth Strickland Keith, who was a pioneer of school desegregation as a student in the 1960s, has served for a number of years on the Franklin County Board of Education, some as chair. Christopher Neal has served on the Louisburg Town Council and came close to being elected mayor in November 2017. On the state level, Dr. Bobbie Richardson, a native of Wood, was appointed to represent North Carolina House District 7, which comprises portions of Franklin and Nash Counties, in 2013.[280]

The eastern Piedmont region has also become a renewed center for Native Americans in the state of North Carolina. Earlier assumptions that the Native Americans had either disappeared completely from the region or died off have been corrected. In 1957, one of the historic groups that lived in the greater Franklin County area, the Saponi, were recognized by the state of North Carolina in the successor Haliwa-Saponi tribe. The Haliwa-Saponi have over four thousand registered members who primarily live in Warren and Halifax Counties, and their population center lies around ten miles from the Franklin County border. Franklin County has a Native American population of 148, and there are frequent efforts to promote native culture and preserve native history at Louisburg College and in local schools.[281]

Despite these changes in business, representation and real estate, Franklin County retains an agricultural character outside of its major towns. The county's landscape is still dominated by large farms. According to a 2017 study by the U.S. Department of Agriculture, the county has 852 agricultural producers who sell around $58 million worth of crops and animal products each year. Tobacco remains the county's largest crop in sales, while nurseries and grains comprise the next-largest crop-growing sectors. Soybeans are the top crop in acreage, a statistic which reflects the general growth in North Carolina soybean production over the past few decades. These numbers remain high relative to other counties, with Franklin County ranking fifty-first in the state in crop production. But the county has dropped substantially from its 2012 numbers, and these will most likely decrease as suburbs and towns in the county continue to grow.[282]

Louisburg's development has contributed to a growing sense of history and commitment to historical preservation in the town. Several ongoing projects, many of which have an association with Louisburg College, have endeavored to tell the town's story. The Person Place Preservation Society, which was operating prior to 1981 and is currently run by Holt Kornegay, tells the story of the Person family and preserves the Person Place House, which is now located on the Louisburg College campus. Across the street, the former Louisburg Male Academy building, which now houses the Tar River Center for History and Culture, still stands. The center, which was founded by Dr. Mark La Branche and run for several years by local historian Maury York, has completed numerous projects related to historic preservation and oral history over the past six years. It has received statewide attention for its large oral history of school desegregation, which it completed in 2015.[283] Other local historians, such as George-Anne Willard Brown and Joe Pearce, have done extensive work on the area's family histories and the history of Louisburg College.

Over the past four decades, Franklin County has reinvented itself like few other counties in the eastern Piedmont region have. Many areas of the county have made closer ties to the large population centers around them; Franklinton and Youngsville continue to open businesses and housing developments dependent on traffic from Raleigh, while Louisburg is tightening its Wake County ties with a long-overdue U.S. 401 road-widening project. But Franklin County refuses to simply become a bedroom community for the Research Triangle Park. It has fostered a host of new businesses and economic areas. Franklin County's unemployment rate had dropped to 3.6 percent as of September 2019—its lowest since 2000.[284] And the county's towns have begun to replace their older businesses. Old mills are becoming apartment buildings, and former warehouses are transitioning to office spaces. Most importantly, the towns and surrounding countryside are developing a new identity, one that will hopefully make the twenty-first century as prosperous and as hopeful for Franklin County as so much of the twentieth century was.

NOTES

Preface

1. Richard Stradling, "Lawmakers Say They Kept US 401 Project on Track. DOT Says Delay Was Never Considered," *News and Observer* (Raleigh, NC), November 26, 2019, www.newsobserver.com.

Chapter 1

2. American FactFinder, "Population, Housing Units, Area, and Density: 2010, North Carolina," www.factfinder.census.gov.
3. The Diggings, "Mining Commodities in Franklin County, North Carolina," www.thediggings.com; Wallace R. Griffitts and Jerry C. Olson, "Mica Deposits of the Southeastern Piedmont." Part 6, Outlying Deposits in North Carolina (Geological Survey Professional Paper 248-D, Washington, D.C.: U.S. Government Printing Office, 1953), 284, www.pubs.usgs.gov.
4. U.S. Climate Data, "Climate Louisburg–North Carolina," www.usclimatedata.com.
5. Megan Funk and Jeroen van den Hurk, "Comprehensive Architectural Survey of Franklin County, North Carolina" (Tarboro, NC: Commonwealth Heritage Group, Inc., April 19, 2018), www.nmcdn.io; J.D. Lewis, "The Moratoc Indians," www.carolana.com; Stephen R. Claggett, "First

Immigrants: Native American Settlements of North Carolina," *Tar Heel Junior Historian* (spring 1995), www.ncpedia.org; Edmund S. Morgan, *American Slavery, American Freedom: The Ordeal of Colonial Virginia* (New York: W.W. Norton and Company, 1975), 52–6.

6. David La Vere, *The Tuscarora War: Indians, Settlers, and the Fight for the Carolina Colonies* (Chapel Hill: University of North Carolina Press, 2013), 44.

7. John Collet, cartographer, *A Compleat Map of North-Carolina from an Actual Survey*, 1770, 70 × 107 cm, North Carolina Maps, www.dc.lib.unc.edu.

8. John Lawson, *A New Voyage to Carolina*, ed. Hugh Talmage Lefler (Chapel Hill: University of North Carolina Press, 1967), 64.

9. Ibid., 65.

10. La Vere, *The Tuscarora War*, 169.

11. T.H. Pearce, *Franklin County, 1779–1979* (Freeman, SD: Pine Hill Press, 1979), vi–vii.

12. Work Projects Administration, *North Carolina: A Guide to the Old North State* (Chapel Hill: University of North Carolina Press, 1939), 93, 346.

13. Mary Beth Fitts, e-mail message to author, February 4, 2019.

14. Hugh Talmage Lefler and William S. Powell, *Colonial North Carolina: A History* (New York: Scribner, 1973), 87, 117.

15. William S. Powell and Michael Hill, *The North Carolina Gazetteer*, 2nd ed. (Chapel Hill: University of North Carolina Press, 2010), 118.

16. Manly Wade Wellman, *The County of Warren, North Carolina, 1586–1917* (Chapel Hill: University of North Carolina Press, 1959), 18–9.

Chapter 2

17. North Carolina Department of Archives and History, National Register of Historic Places nomination form for Cascine, November 2, 1972, www.files.nc.gov.

18. North Carolina Division of Archives and History, National Register of Historic Places nomination form for the Shemuel Kearney House, March 13, 1975, www.files.nc.gov.

19. Chester Paul Middlesworth, "Whiskey," in *Encyclopedia of North Carolina*, ed. William S. Powell (Chapel Hill: University of North Carolina Press, 2006), www.ncpedia.org; Osborn Jeffreys will, dated 1793, Franklin County Wills and Inventories 1785–1797, A:95, www.ncgenweb.us; William Jeffreys will and estate, dated 1803, Franklin County Wills and Inventories, B:69–79, www.ncgenweb.us.

20. Walter Clark, ed., "An Act for Amending an Act, Intituled, An Act for Dividing the Parish of St. John, in Granville County, 1761," in *The State Records of North Carolina*, (Raleigh, NC: P.M. Hale, Printer to the State, 1905), 23:547, www.docsouth.unc.edu.

21. Isaac Edwards, "List of Taxables in North Carolina for the Year 1765," in William Saunders, ed., *Colonial Records of North Carolina*, (Raleigh, NC: P.M. Hale, Printer to the State, 1886), 7:145–6, www.docsouth.unc.edu.

22. William Saunders, ed., "Minutes of the Lower House of the North Carolina General Assembly, November 7, 1764," in *Colonial Records of North Carolina* (Raleigh, NC: P.M. Hale, Printer to the State, 1886), 6:1,273, www.docsouth.unc.edu.

23. John F.D. Smyth, *A Tour of the United States of America* (New York: Arno Press, 1968), 1:113–5, quoted in Alan Watson, ed., *Society in Early North Carolina: A Documentary History* (Raleigh: North Carolina Division of Archives and History, 2010), 93.

24. Letter from Charles Cupples to Daniel Burton, April 25, 1771, in William Saunders, ed., *Colonial Records of North Carolina* (Raleigh, NC: P.M. Hale, Printer to the State, 1886), 8:551–3, www.docsouth.unc.edu.

25. John S. Bassett, "The Regulators of North Carolina," in *Annual Report of the American Historical Association for the Year 1894* (Washington, D.C.: Government Printing Office, 1895), 141–212, www.archive.org; Minutes of the North Carolina Governor's Council, December 4, 1770, in William Saunders, ed., *Colonial Records of North Carolina* (Raleigh, NC: P.M. Hale, Printer to the State, 1886), 8:262, www.docsouth.unc.edu.

26. Marshall De Lancey Haywood, *Governor William Tryon and His Administration in the Province of North Carolina, 1765–1771* (Raleigh, NC: E.M. Uzzell, Printer, 1903), 118, www.archive.org.

27. Hugh F. Rankin, "Jethro Sumner," in *Dictionary of North Carolina Biography*, ed. William S. Powell (Chapel Hill: University of North Carolina Press, 1996), www.ncpedia.org; Armistead Jones Rankin, "Benjamin Hawkins," in *Dictionary of North Carolina Biography*, ed. William S. Powell (Chapel Hill: University of North Carolina Press, 1988), www.ncpedia.org.

28. "Association by Some Inhabitants of Bute County Concerning a Militia for Mutual Self-Defense, [1774?]," in William Saunders, ed., *Colonial Records of North Carolina* (Raleigh, NC: P.M. Hale, Printer to the State, 1886), 9:1104–5, www.docsouth.unc.edu.

29. "Act of the North Carolina General Assembly Concerning Recruitment of Continental Army Troops, April 27, 1778," in William Saunders, ed.,

Colonial Records of North Carolina (Raleigh, NC: P.M. Hale, Printer to the State, 1896), 13:411–7, www.docsouth.unc.edu.

30. Letter from Thomas Sherrod to Richard Caswell, March 22, 1779, in William Saunders, ed., *Colonial Records of North Carolina* (Raleigh, NC: P.M. Hale, Printer to the State, 1896), 14:46, www.docsouth.unc.edu.

31. Benjamin Lee Seawell, *The Genealogy, with Historical and Personal Comments, of the Known Descendants of Col. Benjamin Seawell, Sr., and Lucy Hicks* (South Pasadena, CA: L.C. Mock, Printer, 1935), 6, www.archive.org.

32. Letter from Benjamin Seawell to Abner Nash, July 26, 1780, in William Saunders, ed., *Colonial Records of North Carolina* (Raleigh, NC: P.M. Hale, Printer to the State, 1898), 15:8–9, www.docsouth.unc.edu.

33. Grant to William Sherrard, March 11, 1760, Granville County, 14:67, grant no. 9. Available online at North Carolina Land Grant Images and Data, file no. 932, MARS ID 12.14.66.27, www.nclandgrants.com; Letter from Thomas Sherrod to Richard Caswell, 14:46, www.docsouth.unc. edu; Sherrod Family Papers, 1802–1967 (bulk 1802–65) [finding aid], collection 05206, Southern Historical Collection, University of North Carolina Libraries, Chapel Hill, NC, www.finding-aids.lib.unc.edu.

34. George-Anne Willard, ed., *Franklin County Sketchbook* (Louisburg, NC: Franklin County-Louisburg Bicentenary Committee of the Franklin County Historical Society, 1982), 20.

35. North Carolina Division of Archives and History, National Register of Historic Places nomination form for the Green Hill House, April 8, 1975, www.files.nc.gov.

36. Willard, *Franklin County Sketchbook*, 72.

37. T.N. Ivey, "The Celebrated Conference at Green Hill's," *American Illustrated Methodist Magazine* 6 (September 1901–February 1902), 480; "North Carolina," in Matthew Simpson, ed., *Cyclopedia of Methodism: Embracing Sketches of Its Rise, Progress, and Present Condition* (Philadelphia: Everts and Stewart, 1878), 663.

38. "An Act for Dividing Bute County into Two Distinct Counties and for Other Purposes Therein Mentioned. Acts of the North Carolina General Assembly, 1779," in Walter Clark, ed., *State Records of North Carolina* (Raleigh, NC: P.M. Hale, Printer to the State, 1905), 24:227–30, www.docsouth.unc.edu.

39. Willard, *Franklin County Sketchbook*, 24.

40. "An Act for Dividing Bute County into Two Distinct Counties and for Other Purposes Therein Mentioned. Acts of the North Carolina General Assembly, 1779," in Walter Clark, ed., *State Records of North*

Carolina (Raleigh, NC: P.M. Hale, Printer to the State, 1905), 24:227–30, www.docsouth.unc.edu.

41. Ibid.

Chapter 3

42. "Warren County Census of 1790," in *Colonial Records of North Carolina* 26:1188–204, www.docsouth.unc.edu.

43. "Franklin County Census of 1790," in *Colonial Records of North Carolina* 26:541–55, www.docsouth.unc.edu.

44. North Carolina Division of Archives and History, National Register of Historic Places nomination form for Portridge, January 24, 1990, www.files.nc.gov.

45. North Carolina Division of Archives and History, National Register of Historic Places nomination form for Monreath, June 13, 1975, www.files.nc.gov.

46. Willard, *Franklin County Sketchbook*, 93; North Carolina Department of Archives and History, National Register of Historic Places nomination form for the Person Place, February 1, 1972, www.files.nc.gov.

47. Michael R. Hill, *Historical Research Report: The Person Place of Louisburg, N.C.* (Raleigh: North Carolina Division of Archives and History, 1985), 1:24, www.digital.ncdcr.gov.

48. Ibid., 1:15, 21, 48.

49. North Carolina Division of Archives and History, National Register of Historic Places nomination form for Locust Grove, August 22, 1975, www.files.nc.gov.

50. Alan D. Watson, *Edgecombe County: A Brief History* (Raleigh: Division of Archives and History, North Carolina Department of Cultural Resources, 1979), 14.

51. Pearce, *Franklin County*, 29.

52. North Carolina Division of Archives and History, National Register Nomination of Historic Places nomination form for the Green Hill House, April 8, 1975, www.files.nc.gov.

53. Pearce, *Franklin County*, 6.

54. "An Act to Erect and Establish an Academy in the County of Franklin," in *Colonial Records of North Carolina* 24:876–8, www.docsouth.unc.edu.

55. George-Anne Willard, *Louisburg College Echoes: Voices from the Formative Years, 1787–1917: With a Summary of the Expansion Years, 1917–1987* (Louisburg, NC: Louisburg College, 1988), 16.

56. Charles L. Coon, *North Carolina Schools and Academies, 1790–1840: A Documentary History* (Raleigh, NC: Edwards and Broughton Printing Company, 1915), 84–106.

57. Louisburg College, "Style & Brand," www.louisburg.edu.

58. R.D.W. Connor, ed., *A Manual of North Carolina, Issued by the North Carolina Historical Commission for the Use of Members of the General Assembly, Session 1913* (Raleigh, NC: E.M. Uzzell and Company, State Printers, 1913), 425.

59. McDowell Genealogy, "Green Hill and Grace Bennett," www.mcdowellgenealogy.com.

60. John H. Wheeler, *Historical Sketches of North Carolina: From 1584 to 1851, Compiled from Original Records, Official Documents and Traditional Statements, with Biographical Sketches of Her Distinguished Statemen, Jurists, Lawyers, Soldiers, Divines, Etc.* (Philadelphia: Lippincott, Grambo and Company, 1851), 150.

61. "Journal of the Senate Commencing the 19th November, 1785," in *Colonial Records of North Carolina* 20:34, www.docsouth.unc.edu.

62. Thornton W. Mitchell, "John Haywood," in *Dictionary of North Carolina Biography*, ed. William S. Powell (Chapel Hill: University of North Carolina Press, 1988), www.ncpedia.org.

63. Donald Jackson, ed., *Letters of the Lewis and Clark Expedition with Related Documents, 1783–1854* (Chicago: University of Illinois Press, 1978), 1:365.

64. A.R. Newsome, "Twelve North Carolina Counties in 1810–1811. III. Franklin County," *North Carolina Historical Review* 6, no. 2 (April 1929): 173, www.archive.org.

65. Jonathan Price and John Strother, cartographers, "To David Stone and Peter Brown Esqrs. This First Actual Survey of the State of North Carolina taken by the Subscribers," 1808, 74.29 × 149.86 cm, North Carolina Maps, www.dc.lib.unc.edu.

66. "Diary of Edward Hooker," in *Annual Report of the American Historical Association for the Year 1896* (Washington, D.C.: Government Printing Office, 1896), 1:914.

67. Newsome, "Twelve North Carolina Counties in 1810–1811," 171.

68. "Acts of the North Carolina General Assembly, 1782," in *Colonial Records of North Carolina* 24:449, www.docsouth.unc.edu; "An Act for Impowering the County Courts of Warren and Franklin to Levy a Further Tax on the Inhabitants of Said Counties, for Defraying the Expence of Building a Court House, Prison and Stocks, Acts of the North Carolina General Assembly, 1784," in *Colonial Records of North Carolina* 24:669, www.docsouth.unc.edu.

69. "An Act for Clearing and Opening the Navigation of Tar River and Fishing Creek, Acts of the North Carolina General Assembly, 1784," in *Colonial Records of North Carolina* 24:702, www.docsouth.unc.edu.

70. North Carolina Division of Archives and History, National Register of Historic Places nomination form for the Green Hill House, April 8, 1975, www.files.nc.gov.

71. I. Low and Alexander Anderson, cartographers, "The State of North Carolina from the Best Authorities," 1899, 18.7 × 31.4 cm, North Carolina Maps, www.dc.lib.unc.edu.

72. Mark Murphy, transcriber, "Extract of Minutes, 1791–1800, Franklin County Court Records," Franklin County, NC GenWeb, www.ncgenweb.us; Mark Murphy, transcriber, "Extract of Minutes, 1808–1810, Franklin County Court Records," Franklin County, NC GenWeb, www.ncgenweb.us.

73. "Minutes of the North Carolina House of Commons, October 22 to November 26, 1784," in *Colonial Records of North Carolina* 19:763, 791, www.docsouth.unc.edu.

74. Bob Radcliffe, "Lynch Creek Historic Research Journal," Lynch Creek Farm, www.lynchcreek.com.

75. Diane Taylor Torrent, *Franklin County* (Charleston, SC: Arcadia Publishing, 2014), 24; Pearce, *Franklin County*, 4, 19.

76. David A. Norris, "War of 1812," in *Encyclopedia of North Carolina*, ed. William S. Powell (Chapel Hill: University of North Carolina Press, 2006), www.ncpedia.org.

77. Pearce, *Franklin County*, 38.

78. Michael Hill, "James Turner," in *The Governors of North Carolina* (Raleigh: North Carolina Office of Archives and History, 2007), 142–4.

79. Pearce, *Franklin County*, 42.

80. "An Act for Adding Part of Wake County to Franklin County, Acts of the North Carolina General Assembly, 1786–1787," in *Colonial Records of North Carolina* 24:838, www.docsouth.unc.edu.

81. Richard L. Forstall, *Population of States and Counties of the United States: 1790–1990* (Washington, D.C.: U.S. Bureau of the Census, 1996), 117.

Chapter 4

82. J.D. Lewis, "North Carolina Railroads-Raleigh & Gaston Railroad," www.carolana.com.

83. North Carolina Division of Archives and History, National Register of Historic Places nomination form for the Franklinton Depot, November 14, 1990, www.files.nc.gov.

84. Fletcher Green, "Gold Mining: A Forgotten Industry of Antebellum North Carolina," *North Carolina Historical Review* 14, no. 1 (January 1937): 1–19.

85. George-Anne Willard, ed., "Journal of Nicholas B. Massenberg, Planter, 1839," in *Sketches of Franklin County* (Louisburg, NC: Franklin County-Louisburg Bicentenary Committee, 1982), 43, www.archive.org.

86. North Carolina Highway Historical Marker Program, "Bright Leaf Tobacco," www.ncmarkers.com.

87. Joseph C.G. Kennedy, *Population of the United States in 1860, Compiled from the Original Returns of the Eighth Census* (Washington, D.C.: Government Printing Office, 1864), 348, www2.census.gov.

88. Ibid., 354.

89. E. Hergesheimer, cartographer, "Map Showing the Distribution of the Slave Population of the Southern States of the United States, Compiled from the Census of 1860," September 9, 1861, www.census.gov.

90. Maury York, "James Boon, Free Black Carpenter of Franklin County," *Franklin Times* (Louisburg, NC), January 27, 2016.

91. John Hope Franklin, *The Free Negro in North Carolina, 1790–1860* (New York: W.W. Norton and Company, 1971), 159.

92. William N. Fuller, cartographer, "Township Map of Franklin County, North Carolina," circa 1868, 88 × 64 cm, North Carolina Maps, www.dc.lib.unc.edu.

93. William Thomson, *Thomson's Mercantile and Professional Directory* (Baltimore: William Thomson, 1851), 191.

94. Bureau of the Census, *Manufactures of the United States in 1860, Compiled from the Original Returns of the Eighth Census* (Washington, D.C.: Government Printing Office, 1865), 425, www2.census.gov.

95. Megan Funk and Jeroen van den Hurk, *Comprehensive Architectural Survey of Franklin County, North Carolina* (Tarboro, NC: Commonwealth Heritage Group Inc., April 19, 2018), www.nmcdn.io.

96. Charles L. Coon, *North Carolina Schools and Academies, 1790–1840: A Documentary History* (Raleigh, NC: Edwards and Broughton Printing Company, 1915), 116.

97. North Carolina Division of Archives and History, National Register of Historic Places nomination form for Main Building-Louisburg College, September 14, 1978, www.files.nc.gov.

98. North Carolina Division of Archives and History, National Register of Historic Places nomination form for Speed Farm, November 8, 1991, www.files.nc.gov.

99. North Carolina Division of Archives and History, National Register of Historic Places nomination form for Baker Farm, July 8, 1982, www.files.nc.gov.

100. North Carolina Division of Archives and History, National Register of Historic Places nomination form for the Dr. Samuel Perry House, April 8, 1975, www.files.nc.gov.

101. R.D.W. Connor, ed., *A Manual of North Carolina, Issued by the North Carolina Historical Commission for the Use of Members of the General Assembly, Session 1913* (Raleigh, NC: E.M. Uzzell, 1913), 993, 997.

102. J.D. Lewis, "Franklin County, NC Post Offices-1785 to 1971," www.carolana.com.

103. Atlas Obscura, "Tomb of William Jeffreys, Youngsville, North Carolina," www.atlasobscura.com.

104. Frederick Law Olmstead, *A Journey in the Seaboard Slave States, with Remarks on Their Economy* (New York: Dix and Edwards, 1856), 366, www.docsouth.unc.edu.

105. *Born in Slavery: Slave Narratives from the Federal Writers' Project, 1936–1938*, Vol. 11, North Carolina: Library of Congress, www.loc.gov.

106. Federal Writers' Project of the Works Progress Administration, *Slave Narratives: A Folk History of Slavery in the United States from Interviews with Former Slaves*, Vol. 11, North Carolina Narratives (Washington, D.C.: Works Progress Administration, 1941), 1:19–26 (Mary Anderson), 2:16–6 (Lily Perry), 1:8–12 (Ida Adkins).

107. Daniel R. Goodloe, *Inquiry into the Causes Which Have Retarded the Accumulation of Wealth and Increase of Population in the Southern States: In Which the Question of Slavery Is Considered in a Politico-Economical Point of View. By a Carolinian* (Washington, D.C.: W. Blanchard, 1846), www.docsouth.unc.edu.

108. Biff Hollingsworth, "15 April 1861: You Can Get No Troops from North Carolina…," The Civil War Day by Day, www.blogs.lib.unc.edu.

109. Samuel A'court Ashe, *History of North Carolina* (Raleigh, NC: Edwards and Broughton Printing Company, 1925), 2:544; *Weekly Standard* (Raleigh, NC), "North-Carolina State Convention," May 29, 1861, www.chroniclingamerica.loc.gov.

110. Walter Dean Burnham, *Presidential Ballots, 1836–1892* (Baltimore, MD: Johns Hopkins Press, 1955), 206, www.archive.org.

Chapter 5

111. Hugh T. Lefler, *History of North Carolina* (New York: Lewis Historical Publishing Co., 1956), 2:494.

112. Ibid., 498.

113. T.H. Pearce, *They Fought: The Story of Franklin County Men in the Years 1861–1865* (Chicago: Adams Press, 1969), 5.

114. Walter McKenzie Clark, *History of the Raleigh and Gaston Railroad Company, Including All the Acts of the General Assembly of North Carolina Relating Thereto* (Raleigh, NC: Raleigh News Steam Job Print, 1877), www.docsouth.unc.edu.

115. Raphael Prosper Thian, "Extracts from the Journal of the Confederate Congresses on Legislation Affecting the Flag and Seal," in *Documentary History of the Flag and Seal of the Confederate States of America, 1861–1865* (Washington, D.C.: n.p., 1880), 4–5, www.archive.org.

116. Maury York, "Abby House," in *Dictionary of North Carolina Biography*, ed. William S. Powell (Chapel Hill: University of North Carolina, 1988), 3:210, www.ncpedia.org.

117. Edward Robins, *William T. Sherman* (Philadelphia: G.W. Jacobs, 1905), 310, www.archive.org; William T. Sherman, *General Sherman's Official Account of His Great March Through Georgia and the Carolinas* (New York: Bunce and Huntington, 1865), 122–3, www.archive.org.

118. Anna Long Thomas Fuller, *Anna Long Thomas Fuller's Journal, 1856–1890: A Civil War Diary*, ed. Myrtle C. King (Alpharetta, GA: Priority Pub, 1999), 43.

119. Ibid., 46.

120. Ibid., 48.

121. Federal Writers' Project, *Slave Narratives*, 1:25.

122. Ibid., 1:218–21.

123. Ibid., 2:231.

124. North Carolina Highway Historical Marker Program, "Freedmen's Convention," www.ncmarkers.com.

125. John Haley, *Charles N. Hunter and Race Relations in North Carolina* (Chapel Hill: University of North Carolina Press, 1987), 32, 40.

126. John L. Cheney Jr., ed., *North Carolina Government, 1585–1979: A Narrative and Statistical History* (Raleigh: North Carolina Department of the Secretary of State, 1981), 845, www.archive.org.

127. James L. Leloudis, "Civil War and Reconstruction," in *The First Century of the First State University* (Chapel Hill, NC: University of Chapel Hill), www.docsouth.unc.edu.

128. Ibid.

129. Funk, *Comprehensive Architectural Survey of Franklin County*.

130. *Report on the Manufactures of the United States at the Tenth Census (June 1, 1880)* (Washington, D.C.: Government Printing House, 1883), 2:318, www2.census.gov.

131. E.T. Malone Jr., "Edwin Wiley Fuller," in *Dictionary of North Carolina Biography*, ed. William S. Powell (Chapel Hill: University of North Carolina Press, 1986), 2:248–9, www.ncpedia.org.

132. "Literary: 'The Angel in the Cloud,'" *Franklin Courier* (Louisburg, NC), July 4, 1873, www.newspapers.com.

133. W.J. Peele and Clarence Poe, ed., *Historical and Literary Activities in North Carolina, 1900–1905* (Goldsboro, NC: Nash Bros., 1904), 69–70.

134. "Senate, Saturday, August 8, 1868," *Wilmington (NC) Journal*, August 14, 1868, www.chroniclingamerica.loc.gov.

135. "Riot at Louisburg," *Wilmington (NC) Journal*, July 23, 1869, www.chroniclingamerica.loc.gov.

136. W.W. Holden, *Trial of William W. Holden, Governor of North Carolina, Before the Senate of North Carolina* (Raleigh, NC: Sentinel Printing House, 1871), 3: 2, 558–63, www.archive.org.

137. R.D.W. Connor, ed., *A Manual of North Carolina, Issued by the North Carolina Historical Commission for the Use of Members of the General Assembly, Session 1913* (Raleigh, NC: E.M. Uzzell and Company, State Printers, 1913), 1,001.

138. "Our Rocky Mount Correspondence," *Tarboro Southerner* (Tarboro, NC), August 27, 1868, www.chroniclingamerica.loc.gov.

139. Maury York, "Abby House," in *Dictionary of North Carolina Biography*, ed. William S. Powell (Chapel Hill: University of North Carolina, 1988), 3:210, www.ncpedia.org.

140. J.J. de Roulhac Hamilton, *Reconstruction in North Carolina* (New York: Columbia University Press, 1914), 247–8, 405, www.archive.org.

141. Cong. Globe, 41st Cong., 2d Sess. 102 (1870).

Chapter 6

142. Lefler, *History of North Carolina*, 2:664–8.

143. Pearce, *Franklin County*, 82.

144. Norman C. Larson, "Review of *Zeb's Black Baby, Vance County, North Carolina*, by Samuel Thomas Peace," *North Carolina Historical Review* 33, no. 2 (April 1956), 257–8.

145. James C. Burke, "North Carolina's First Railroads, A Study in Historical Geography" (PhD diss., University of North Carolina at Greensboro, 2008), www.libres.uncg.edu; "House of Representatives," *Wilmington (NC) Journal*, April 2, 1869, www.chroniclingamerica.loc.gov; "The Legislature," *Weekly North-Carolina Standard* (Raleigh, NC), March 31, 1869, www.chroniclingamerica.loc.gov.

146. Funk, *Comprehensive Architectural Survey of Franklin County*.

147. "Talk of the Town," *The Gold Leaf* (Henderson, NC), November 5, 1896, www.chroniclingamerica.loc.gov.

148. "Louisburg," *Weekly North-Carolina Standard* (Raleigh, NC), March 24, 1869, www.chroniclingamerica.loc.gov.

149. Jacob and George Chace, cartographers, "Gray's New Map of Louisburg, Franklin County, North Carolina," circa 1882, 70 × 35 cm, North Carolina Maps, www.dc.lib.unc.edu.

150. W.S. Mitchell, "A High and Gay Time in Louisburg—A Regular Jollification Celebration Among the Republicans—Men, Women and Children Turned Out—A Perfectly Harmonious Affair over the Grand Republican Victory on the 3[d] of November," *Gazette* (Raleigh, NC), November 28, 1896, www.chroniclingamerica.loc.gov.

151. National Register of Historic Places nomination form for the Franklinton Depot, November 14, 1990, www.files.nc.gov.

152. Pearce, *Franklin County*, 91.

153. Levis Branson, ed., *Branson's North Carolina Business Directory, 1896* (Raleigh, NC: Levi Branson, 1896), 280, 282.

154. United States Census Bureau, "Agriculture—Cotton Production. North Carolina, South Carolina, Georgia, Florida," in *Census Bulletin* no. 190 (N.p.: June 2, 1892), www.census.gov.

155. National Register of Historic Places nomination form for Sterling Cotton Mill, April 10, 1996, www.files.nc.gov.

156. Funk, *Comprehensive Architectural Survey of Franklin County*.

157. J.D. Lewis, "Franklin County, NC Post Offices-1785 to 1971," www.carolana.com.

158. Levi Branson, ed., *Branson's North Carolina Business Directory, 1896* (Raleigh, NC: Levi Branson, 1896), 280.

159. Lewis, "Franklin County, NC Post Offices-1785 to 1971."

160. National Register of Historic Places nomination form for Louisburg Historic District, December 11, 1986, www.files.nc.gov.

161. Ibid.

162. Sarah Zielinski, "Strange Rain: Why Fish, Frogs and Golf Balls Fall from the Skies," *Smithsonian Magazine*, September 8, 2015, www.smithsonianmag.com; Pearce, *Franklin County*, 205–7.

163. Willard, *Louisburg College*, 85.

164. Ibid., 92.

165. "The Commencements," *Progressive Farmer* (Winston, NC), June 5, 1900, www.chroniclingamerica.loc.gov.

166. G.F. Richings, *Evidences of Progress Among Colored People* (Philadelphia: G.S. Ferguson Co., 1902), 176, www.docsouth.unc.edu.

167. Funk, *Comprehensive Architectural Survey of Franklin County*.

168. "How the Work Is Progressing," *Progressive Farmer* (Winston, NC), December 22, 1887, www.chroniclingamerica.loc.gov.

169. "Piny [sic] Grove Alliance, No. 214, Louisburg, N.C., Dec. 17, '88," *Progressive Farmer* (Winston, NC), January 22, 1889, www.chroniclingamerica.loc.gov.

170. Connor, *A Manual of North Carolina*, 1,005.

171. "The Legislature," *Gazette* (Raleigh, NC), November 28, 1896, www.chroniclingamerica.loc.gov.

172. University of North Carolina, "NC Jim Crow Laws 1899–1919," Digital Humanities History and Methods, www.nc-jim-crow-laws.prospect.unc.edu.

173. "How the Counties Voted," *Farmer and Mechanic* (Raleigh, NC), November 13, 1900, www.chroniclingamerica.loc.gov.

174. *News and Observer, North Carolina Year Book, 1901* (Raleigh, NC: *News and Observer*, 1901), 44, www.archive.org.

175. "State Press," *Semi-Weekly Messenger* (Wilmington, NC), March 13, 1900, www.chroniclingamerica.loc.gov.

176. University of North Carolina, "NC Jim Crow Laws 1899–1919."

Chapter 7

177. Funk, *Comprehensive Architectural Survey of Franklin County*.

178. *News and Observer, North Carolina Year Book, 1910* (Raleigh, NC: *News and Observer*, 1910), 209–10, www.archive.org.

179. North Carolina State Highway Commission, "Highway Map of North Carolina Prepared by the North Carolina State Highway Commission for the Five Year Federal Aid Program," 1918, 22.6 × 31.3 cm, North Carolina Maps, www.dc.lib.unc.edu.

180. *News and Observer, North Carolina Year Book 1916* (Raleigh, NC: *News and Observer*, 1916), 238–42, www.archive.org.

181. National Register of Historic Places nomination form for Louisburg Historic District, December 11, 1986, www.files.nc.gov.

182. Ibid.

183. North Carolina Division of Archives and History, National Register of Historic Places nomination form for the Dr. J.H. Harris House, June 2, 1975, www.files.nc.gov.

184. North Carolina Department of Cultural Resources, National Register of Historic Places listing for the C.L. and Bessie G. McGhee House, September 5, 2017, www.files.nc.gov.

185. North Carolina Division of Archives and History, National Register of Historic Places nomination form for the Andrews-Moore House, November 4, 1998, www.files.nc.gov.

186. Funk, *Comprehensive Architectural Survey of Franklin County*.

187. *News and Observer, North Carolina Year Book and Business Directory, 1915* (Raleigh, NC: *News and Observer*, 1915), 217, www.archive.org.

188. Pearce, *Franklin County*, 137.

189. Louisburg College, *Catalogue of Officers, Teachers and Students 1918–1919; Announcements for 1919–1920* (Raleigh, NC: Edwards & Broughton, Printers, 1929), 11, www.archive.org.

190. Ibid., 48–9.

191. Ibid., 26.

192. *News and Observer, North Carolina Year Book and Business Directory, 1916* (Raleigh, NC: *News and Observer*, 1916), 238, www.archive.org.

193. Maury York, "Great Depression Closed Franklinton Christian College," *Franklin Times* (Louisburg, NC), May 24, 2017.

194. *News and Observer, North Carolina Year Book and Business Directory, 1916*, 239.

195. Ibid., 237.

196. Ibid., 237–8.

197. J.D. Lewis, "North Carolina State House of Representatives, 1901," www.carolana.com; National Register of Historic Places nomination form for Louisburg Historic District, December 11, 1986, www.files.nc.gov.

198. Bickett for Governor Club of Franklin County, *Bickett for Governor: The Record Is the Reason* (Louisburg, NC: Bickett for Governor Club of Franklin County, 1915), www.archive.org.

199. Thomas Walter Bickett, "Biennial Message to the General Assembly, Session 1919," in *Public Letters and Papers of Thomas Walter Bickett, Governor of North Carolina, 1917–1921*, comp. Santford Martin, ed. R.B. House (Raleigh, NC: Edwards and Broughton Printing Company, 1923), 26, www.archive.org.

200. Ibid., 27.

201. Pearce, *Franklin County*, 152.

202. W.J. Cash, *The Mind of the South*, repr. (1941; repr. New York, NY: Vintage Books, 1991), 292.

203. Cash, *The Mind of the South*, 294.

204. University of North Carolina, "Confederate Monument, Louisburg," Commemorative Landscapes, www.docsouth.unc.edu.

205. University of North Carolina, "First Confederate Flag and Its Designer O.R. Smith, Louisburg," Commemorative Landscapes, www.docsouth.unc.edu.

206. "White People of Franklin County: Its [sic] Your Time to Act—Go to the Polls and Vote for White Supremacy," *Franklin Times* (Louisburg, NC), October 29, 1920, www.newspapers.digitalnc.org.

207. Elijah Gaddis and Seth Kotch, "Walter Tyler," in *A Red Record: Revealing Lynching Sites in North Carolina* (Chapel Hill: University of North Carolina), www.lynching.web.unc.edu.

208. Ibid., "Powell Green"; "Whole State Shocked and Humiliated Says Bickett, on Lynching," *Greensboro Daily News*, December 29, 1919.

209. State Superintendent of Public Instruction, *Directory of the School Officials of North Carolina, October, 1921* (Raleigh, NC: North Carolina Department of Public Instruction), 12, www.archive.org.

210. Funk, *Comprehensive Architectural Survey of Franklin County*.

Chapter 8

211. Department of Conservation and Development, *North Carolina: The Pacemaker in Industry, Agriculture and Substantial Progress* (Raleigh, NC: Observer Printing House, 1926), 11, www.archive.org.

212. NCRoads.com Annex, "N.C. 56," www.vahighways.com.

213. North Carolina State Highway Commission, "North Carolina County Road Survey of Franklin County," 1930, 35.6 × 36.3 cm, North Carolina Maps, www.dc.lib.unc.edu; NCRoads.com Annex, "N.C. 561," www.vahighways.com.

214. Funk, *Comprehensive Architectural Survey of Franklin County*.

215. *News and Observer, North Carolina Year Book, 1923* (Raleigh, NC: *News and Observer*, 1923), 56, www.archive.org.

216. J.D. Lewis, "North Carolina State House of Representatives, 1921," "North Carolina State House of Representatives, 1925" and "North Carolina State House of Representatives, 1927," www.carolana.com.

217. FamilySearch, "United States Census, 1910, North Carolina > Franklin > Youngsville > ED 32 > image 2 of 36," www.familysearch.org, citing NARA microfilm publication T624 (Washington, D.C.: National Archives and Records Administration, n.d.).

218. Willard, *Franklin County Sketchbook*, 140.

219. "Franklin County Observes 150th Birthday," *Franklin Times* (Louisburg, NC), July 12, 1929, www.newspapers.digitalnc.org.

220. Contract between Edward and Maria Alston, parties of the first part, and P.G. Alston and D.T. Smithwick, parties of the second part, dated July 26, 1900, D.T. Smithwick Collection, PC.257, Gold Mine Land Folder, State Archives of North Carolina, Raleigh, NC.

221. Ethel W. Twiford, ed., *Do All Things with a Single Eye to the Glory of God: A History of Saint Paul United Methodist Church, Goldsboro, North Carolina* (Goldsboro, NC: Hilburn Printing Corporation, 1983), 95.

222. Josephus Daniels, *Biennial Report of the Superintendent of Public Instruction of North Carolina for the Scholastic Years 1891 and 1892* (Raleigh, NC: Department of Public Instruction, 1893), 68.

223. Lefler, *History of North Carolina*, 2:795.

224. North Carolina State Highway Commission, "North Carolina County Road Survey of Franklin County," 1930, 35.6 × 36.3 cm, North Carolina Maps, www.dc.lib.unc.edu.

225. *News and Observer, North Carolina Year Book, 1923*, 72.

226. Funk, *Comprehensive Architectural Survey of Franklin County*.

227. Louisburg College, *Louisburg College Catalogue 1938–1939* (Louisburg, NC: Louisburg College, 1938), 56, www.archive.org.

228. Ibid., 8.

229. Funk, *Comprehensive Architectural Survey of Franklin County*.

230. National Register of Historic Places nomination form for Louisburg Historic District, December 11, 1986, www.files.nc.gov.

231. Funk, *Comprehensive Architectural Survey of Franklin County*.

232. Gaddis and Seth, "The People," in *A Red Record*.

233. Cash, *The Mind of the South*, 300; Gaddis and Kotch, "Govan Ward," in *A Red Record*.

234. Legal notices, *Franklin Times* (Louisburg, NC), December 27, 1929, www.newspapers.digitalnc.org; Kay Whatley, "From Railroads to Highways: The Bunn Story," *Gray Area News* (Eastern NC), January 25, 2017, www.greyareanews.com.

235. North Carolina Historical Commission, *North Carolina Manual, Issued by the North Carolina Historical Commission for the Use of Members of the*

General Assembly, 1933 (Raleigh: North Carolina Historical Commission, 1933), 89.

236. North Carolina Department of Cultural Resources, National Register of Historic Places listing for the Perry School, January 3, 2011, www.files.nc.gov.

237. "Louisburg Wins 15 out of 17," *Franklin Times* (Louisburg, NC), May 21, 1954, www.newspapers.digitalnc.org.

238. "Town Commissioners Settle Differences," *Franklin Times* (Louisburg, NC), December 12, 1941, www.newspapers.digitalnc.org.

239. "Franklin County Getting in Scrap," *Franklin Times* (Louisburg, NC), October 9, 1942, www.newspapers.digitalnc.org.

240. Pearce, *Franklin County*, 203.

241. Mary Estelle Winston of Youngsville, "Franklin County Girl Enlists in the WAVES," *Franklin Times* (Louisburg, NC), October 9, 1942, www.newspapers.digitalnc.org; "Called for Training," *Franklin Times* (Louisburg, NC), December 11, 1942, www.newspapers.digitalnc.org; Priscilla P. Parrish of Louisburg, "Officer Training," *Franklin Times* (Louisburg, NC), November 5, 1943, www.newspapers.digitalnc.org.

242. Maria Höhn, "African-American GIs of WWII: Fighting for Democracy Abroad and at Home," *Military Times*, January 30, 2018, www.militarytimes.com.

Chapter 9

243. Lefler, *History of North Carolina*, 2:798.

244. North Carolina Secretary of State, *North Carolina State Manual, 1949* (Raleigh, NC: North Carolina Historical Commission, 1949), 200.

245. Margaret Holmes, *A History of the Town of Bunn* (Bunn, NC: Self-pub., 1992), 4.

246. Scott Mason, *Tar Heel Traveler Eats: Food Journeys Across North Carolina* (Guilford, CT: Globe Pequot, 2014), 63–6.

247. Sunrise Biscuit Kitchen, "Recognition and Awards," www.sunrisebiscuits.com.

248. "Special 100th Anniversary Issue," *Franklin Times* (Louisburg, NC), July 30, 1970, 18; Diane Taylor Torrent, *Franklin County* (Charleston, SC: Arcadia Publishing, 2014), 53.

249. Maury York, "County Residents United to Build First Hospital," *Franklin Times* (Louisburg, NC), October 28, 2015.

250. "Ground Broken for Franklin County's Memorial Hospital," *Nashville Graphic* (Nashville, NC), April 21, 1949.

251. William C. Hunt, *Twelfth Census of the United States, Taken in the Year 1900, Population, Part 1* (Washington, D.C.: Government Printing Office, 1901), 1:732–5, www2.census.gov; William C. Hunt, *Fourteenth Census of the United States Taken in the Year 1920* (Washington, D.C.: Government Printing Office, 1922), 3:730, www2.census.gov.

252. *Biennial Report of the Department of Labor, July 1, 1962 to June 30, 1964* (Raleigh: North Carolina Department of Labor), 17.

253. Carey Johnson, "Wilbur Jolly Served Public to Help Others," *Franklin Times* (Louisburg, NC), August 21, 2007.

254. Willard, *Franklin County Sketchbook*, 120.

255. "Former Top Aide to Jesse Helms Dies at Age 72," *Greensboro News and Record*, February 7, 1993, www.greensboro.com.

256. Maury York, "County Schools Were Desegregated 50 Years Ago," *Franklin Times* (Louisburg, NC), March 28, 2018.

257. Richard Hatch, "'Louisburg Incident' Had Nationwide Repercussion," *Kannapolis Daily Independent*, May 19, 1966.

258. Molly McDonough, "Making Brown Real," *American Bar Association Journal*, April 1, 2014, www.abajournal.com.

259. York, "County Schools Were Desegregated 50 Years Ago."

260. "Rosanell Eaton, Fierce Voting Rights Advocate, Dies at 97," *New York Times*, December 9, 2018, www.nytimes.com.

261. North Carolina Secretary of State, *North Carolina Manual, 1960* (Raleigh, NC: North Carolina Historical Commission, 1960), 227–9.

Chapter 10

262. Pearce, *Franklin County*, 262.

263. Duke University Center on Globalization, Governance and Competitiveness at the Social Science Research Institute, "Workers and Wages," North Carolina in the Global Economy, www.ncglobaleconomy.com.

264. Amanda Jones Hoyle, "HON Furniture Plant in Louisburg Closing, Costing 93 Jobs," *Triangle Business Journal*, July 24, 2009, www.bizjournals.com.

265. Susan Folk Dobie, "Too Old for School and Too Young for Social Security: Franklinton Cotton Mill Closes Doors for Last Time," *Franklin Times* (Louisburg, NC), January 16, 1991.

266. Patrick McHugh, "North Carolina's Small Towns and Cities Continue to Experience Weak Labor Markets, *Prosperity Watch* 55, no. 1 (2015), www.ncjustice.org.

267. Ballotpedia, "Lucy Allen," www.ballotpedia.org.

268. North Carolina State Board of Elections, "Voter Registration Statistics for February 16, 2019, Franklin County," www.vt.ncsbe.gov.

269. Louisburg College, "Lou-U Ends Presidential Search with May," *Columns* (Louisburg College, Louisburg, NC), September 1, 1992, www.newspapers.digitalnc.org.

270. Louisburg College, *2018–2019 Louisburg College Catalog* (Louisburg, NC: Louisburg College, 2018), www.louisburg.edu.

271. Vance-Granville Community College, *2019–2020 Student Catalog* (Henderson, NC: Vance-Granville Community College, 2019), www.vgcc.edu.

272. *US News and World Report*, "Vance-Granville Community College: Overview," www.usnews.com.

273. Vance-Granville Community College, "VGCC-Spring Schedule," www.vgcc.edu.

274. North Carolina Department of Commerce, Rural Economic Division, Main Street and Rural Planning Center, *Town of Franklinton, North Carolina, Economic Development Strategic Five-Year Plan, 2019–2023* (Raleigh, NC: Town of Franklinton, March 2019), www.cms5.revize.com.

275. Pearce, *Franklin County*, 244.

276. "Franklin," *The State* 46, no. 8 (January 1979), 35.

277. "NC Community Has No Traffic Laws," *WRAL*, May 13, 1997, www.wral.com.

278. Craig Jarvis, "Home Prices on NC Lakes Are Up. Here's Where They've Soared, and What's 'Affordable,'" *News and Observer* (Raleigh, NC), September 7, 2018, www.newsobserver.com.

279. Support Black Owned, "Hardy Smiles Family Dentistry," www.supportblackowned.com.

280. Bobbie Richardson, NC House, "Dr. Bobbie Richardson, a Lifelong Educator," www.bobbie4nc.com.

281. Gary Cunard, "Echoes of the Past Help Shape Today's World," *Franklin Times* (Louisburg, NC), December 13, 2017; Darian Woehr, "Still Here: The Haliwa-Saponi Fight to Revive Their Language," *MediaHub*, April 30, 2019, www.mediahub.unc.edu.

282. United States Department of Agriculture, "County Profile: Franklin County, North Carolina," 2017 Census of Agriculture, www.nass.usda.gov.

283. Reema Khrais, "Remembering the Fight for School Desegregation in Franklin County," *WUNC*, November 30, 2015, www.wunc.org.

284. Federal Reserve Bank of St. Louis, "U.S. Bureau of Labor Statistics, Unemployment Rate in Franklin County, NC (NCFRAN9URN)," www.fred.stlouisfed.org.

INDEX

ABOUT THE AUTHOR

Eric Medlin is a history instructor at Wake Technical Community College in Raleigh, North Carolina. Eric graduated in 2017 with a master's degree in history from North Carolina State University. He has written on mid-twentieth-century historians, North Carolina monuments and the Kellogg-Briand Pact. Eric is currently working on various state and local history projects. In his spare time, Eric enjoys traveling to small towns and sampling their cuisines.